By *ALDOUS HUXLEY*

Novels
CROME YELLOW
ANTIC HAY
THOSE BARREN LEAVES
POINT COUNTER POINT
BRAVE NEW WORLD
EYELESS IN GAZA
AFTER MANY A SUMMER
TIME MUST HAVE A STOP

Short Stories
LIMBO *
MORTAL COILS
LITTLE MEXICAN
TWO OR THREE GRACES
BRIEF CANDLES

Biography
GREY EMINENCE

Essays and Belles Lettres
ON THE MARGIN
ALONG THE ROAD
PROPER STUDIES
DO WHAT YOU WILL
MUSIC AT NIGHT &
VULGARITY IN LITERATURE
TEXTS AND PRETEXTS (Anthology)
THE OLIVE TREE
ENDS AND MEANS (An Enquiry
into the Nature of Ideals) *
THE ART OF SEEING
THE PERENNIAL PHILOSOPHY

Travel
JESTING PILATE (Illustrated)
BEYOND THE MEXIQUE BAY (Illustrated)

Poetry and Drama
VERSES AND A COMEDY *
(including early poems, Leda, The Cicadas
and The World of Light, a Comedy)

* *Issued in this Collected Edition 1946*

ALDOUS HUXLEY

Verses & A Comedy

Early poems, Leda, The Cicadas,
The World of Light

1946
Chatto & Windus
LONDON

PUBLISHED BY

Chatto & Windus

LONDON

*

Oxford University Press

TORONTO

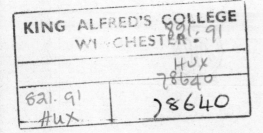
LEDA

FIRST PUBLISHED 1920

SELECTED POEMS

FIRST PUBLISHED 1925

THE CICADAS & THE WORLD OF LIGHT

FIRST PUBLISHED 1931

VERSES & A COMEDY

FIRST ISSUED IN THIS COLLECTED

EDITION 1946

PRINTED IN GREAT BRITAIN

NOTE

The 22 poems included in the Section 'Early Poems' have been chosen by the Author from *Selected Poems*, published by Basil Blackwell, to whom grateful acknowledgments are due for permission to reprint in this volume.

CONTENTS

EARLY POEMS

LEDA

LEDA (*contd.*)

THE CICADAS

THE CICADAS (contd.)

THE WORLD OF LIGHT

EARLY POEMS

SONG OF POPLARS

SHEPHERD, to yon tall poplars tune your flute:
Let them pierce, keenly, subtly shrill,
The slow blue rumour of the hill;
Let the grass cry with an anguish of evening gold,
And the great sky be mute.

Then hearken how the poplar trees unfold
Their buds, yet close and gummed and blind,
In airy leafage of the mind,
Rustling in silvery whispers the twin-hued scales
That fade not nor grow old.

"Poplars and fountains and you cypress spires
Springing in dark and rusty flame,
Seek you aught that hath a name?
Or say, say: Are you all an upward agony
Of undefined desires?

"Say, are you happy in the golden march
Of sunlight all across the day?
Or do you watch the uncertain way
That leads the withering moon on cloudy stairs
Over the heaven's wide arch?

"Is it towards sorrow or towards joy you lift
The sharpness of your trembling spears?
Or do you seek, through the grey tears
That blur the sky, in the heart of the triumphing blue,
A deeper, calmer rift?"

So; I have tuned my music to the trees,
And there were voices dim below
Their shrillness, voices swelling slow
In the blue murmur of hills, and a golden cry
And then vast silences.

THE REEF

My green aquarium of phantom fish,
Goggling in on me through the misty panes;
My rotting leaves and fields spongy with rains;
My few clear quiet autumn days—I wish

I could leave all, clearness and mistiness;
Sodden or goldenly crystal, all too still.
Yes, and I too rot with the leaves that fill
The hollows in the woods; I am grown less

Than human, listless, aimless as the green
Idiot fishes of my aquarium,
Who loiter down their dim tunnels and come
And look at me and drift away, nought seen

Or understood, but only glazedly
Reflected. Upwards, upwards through the shadows,
Through the lush sponginess of deep-sea meadows
Where hare-lipped monsters batten, let me ply

Winged fins, bursting this matrix dark to find
Jewels and movement, mintage of sunlight
Scattered largely by the profuse wind,
And gulfs of blue brightness, too deep for sight.

Free, newly born, on roads of music and air
Speeding and singing, I shall seek the place
Where all the shining threads of water race,
Drawn in green ropes and foamy meshes.   There,

On the red fretted ramparts of a tower
Of coral rooted in the depths, shall break
An endless sequence of joy and speed and power:
Green shall shatter to foam; flake with white flake

Shall create an instant's shining constellation
Upon the blue; and all the air shall be
Full of a million wings that swift and free
Laugh in the sun, all power and strong elation.

Yes, I shall seek that reef, which is beyond
All isles however magically sleeping
In tideless seas, uncharted and unconned
Save by blind eyes: beyond the laughter and weeping

That brood like a cloud over the lands of men.
Movement, passion of colour and pure wings,
Curving to cut like knives—these are the things
I search for:—passion beyond the ken

Of our foiled violences, and, more swift
Than any blow which man aims against time,
The invulnerable, motion that shall rift
All dimness with the lightning of a rhyme,

Or note, or colour.   And the body shall be
Quick as the mind; and will shall find release

From bondage to brute things; and joyously
Soul, will and body, in the strength of triune peace,

Shall live the perfect grace of power unwasted.
And love consummate, marvellously blending
Passion and reverence in a single spring
Of quickening force, till now never yet tasted,

But ever ceaselessly thirsted for, shall crown
The new life with its ageless starry fire.
I go to seek that reef, far down, far down
Below the edge of everyday's desire,

Beyond the magical islands, where of old
I was content, dreaming, to give the lie
To misery.   They were all strong and bold
That thither came; and shall I dare to try?

THE ELMS

FINE as the dust of plumy fountains blowing
Across the lanterns of a revelling night,
The tiny leaves of April's earliest growing
Powder the trees—so vaporously light,
They seem to float, billows of emerald foam
Blown by the South on its bright airy tide,
Seeming less trees than things beatified,
Come from the world of thought which was their
     home.

For a while only.   Rooted strong and fast,
Soon will they lift towards the summer sky
Their mountain-mass of clotted greenery.
Their immaterial season quickly past,
They grow opaque, and therefore needs must die,
Since every earth to earth returns at last.

OUT OF THE WINDOW

In the middle of countries, far from hills and sea,
Are the little places one passes by in trains
And never stops at; where the skies extend
Uninterrupted, and the level plains
Stretch green and yellow and green without an end.
And behind the glass of their Grand Express
Folk yawn away a province through,
With nothing to think of, nothing to do,
Nothing even to look at—never a "view"
In this damned wilderness.
But I look out of the window and find
Much to satisfy the mind.
Mark how the furrows, formed and wheeled
In a motion orderly and staid,
Sweep, as we pass, across the field
Like a drilled army on parade.
And here's a market-garden, barred
With stripe on stripe of varied greens . . .
Bright potatoes, flower starred,
And the opacous colour of beans.

Each line deliberately swings
Towards me, till I see a straight
Green avenue to the heart of things,
The glimpse of a sudden opened gate
Piercing the adverse walls of fate . . .
A moment only, and then, fast, fast,
The gate swings to, the avenue closes;
Fate laughs, and once more interposes
Its barriers.
                    The train has passed.

ANNIVERSARIES

ONCE more the windless days are here,
Quiet of autumn, when the year
Halts and looks backward and draws breath
Before it plunges into death.
Silver of mist and gossamers,
Through-shine of noonday's glassy gold,
Pale blue of skies, where nothing stirs
Save one blanched leaf, weary and old,
That over and over slowly falls
From the mute elm-trees, hanging on air
Like tattered flags along the walls
Of chapels deep in sunlit prayer.
Once more . . . Within its flawless glass
To-day reflects that other day,
When, under the bracken, on the grass,
We who were lovers happily lay

And hardly spoke, or framed a thought
That was not one with the calm hills
And crystal sky.   Ourselves were nought,
Our gusty passions, our burning wills
Dissolved in boundlessness, and we
Were almost bodiless, almost free.

The wind has shattered silver and gold;
Night after night of sparkling cold,
Orion lifts his tangled feet
From where the tossing branches beat
In a fine surf against the sky.
So the trance ended, and we grew
Restless, we knew not how or why;
And there were sudden gusts that blew
Our dreaming banners into storm;
We wore the uncertain crumbling form
Of a brown swirl of windy leaves,
A phantom shape that stirs and heaves
Shuddering from earth, to fall again
With a dry whisper of withered rain.

Last, from the dead and shrunken days
We conjured spring, lighting the blaze
Of burnished tulips in the dark;
And from black frost we struck a spark
Of blue delight and fragrance new,
A little world of flowers and dew.
Winter for us was over and done:
The drought of fluttering leaves had grown
Emerald shining in the sun,
As light as glass, as firm as stone.

Real once more: for we had passed
Through passion into thought again;
Shaped our desires and made that fast
Which was before a cloudy pain;
Moulded the dimness, fixed, defined
In a fair statue, strong and free,
Twin bodies flaming into mind,
Poised on the brink of ecstasy.

ITALY

THERE is a country in my mind,
Lovelier than a poet blind
Could dream of, who had never known
This world of drought and dust and stone
In all its ugliness: a place
Full of an all but human grace;
Whose dells retain the printed form
Of heavenly sleep, and seem yet warm
From some pure body newly risen;
Where matter is no more a prison,
But freedom for the soul to know
Its native beauty.   For things glow
There with an inward truth and are
All fire and colour like a star.
And in that land are domes and towers
That hang as light and bright as flowers
Upon the sky, and seem a birth
Rather of air than solid earth.

Sometimes I dream that walking there
In the green shade, all unaware
At a new turn of the golden glade,
I shall see her, and as though afraid
Shall halt a moment and almost fall
For passing faintness, like a man
Who feels the sudden spirit of Pan
Brimming his narrow soul with all
The illimitable world. And she,
Turning her head, will let me see
The first sharp dawn of her surprise
Turning to welcome in her eyes.
And I shall come and take my lover
And looking on her re-discover
All her beauty:—her dark hair
And the little ears beneath it, where
Roses of lucid shadow sleep;
Her brooding mouth, and in the deep
Wells of her eyes reflected stars.

Oh, the imperishable things
That hands and lips as well as words
Shall speak! Oh movement of white wings,
Oh wheeling galaxies of birds!

BY THE FIRE

WE who are lovers sit by the fire,
Cradled warm 'twixt thought and will,
Sit and drowse like sleeping dogs

In the equipoise of all desire,
Sit and listen to the still
Small hiss and whisper of green logs
That burn away, that burn away
With the sound of a far-off falling stream
Of threaded water blown to steam,
Grey ghost in the mountain world of grey.
Vapours blue as distance rise
Between the hissing logs that show
A glimpse of rosy heat below;
And candles watch with tireless eyes
While we sit drowsing here.   I know,
Dimly, that there exists a world,
That there is time perhaps, and space
Other and wider than this place,
Where at the fireside drowsily curled
We hear the whisper and watch the flame
Burn blinkless and inscrutable.
And then I know those other names
That through my brain from cell to cell
Echo—reverberated shout
Of waiters mournful along corridors:
But nobody carries the orders out,
And the names (dear friends, your name and yours)
Evoke no sign.   But here I sit
On the wide hearth, and there are you:
That is enough and only true.
The world and the friends that lived in it
Are shadows: you alone remain
Real in this drowsing room,
Full of the whispers of distant rain
And candles staring into the gloom.

VALEDICTORY

I HAD remarked—how sharply one observes
When life is disappearing round the curves
Of yet another corner, out of sight!—
I had remarked when it was "good luck" and "good
     night"
And "a good journey to you," on her face
Certain enigmas penned in the hieroglyphs
Of that half frown and queer fixed smile and trace
Of clouded thought in those brown eyes,
Always so happily clear of hows and ifs—
My poor bleared mind!—and haunting whys.

There I stood, holding her farewell hand,
(Pressing my life and soul and all
The world to one good-bye, till, small
And smaller pressed, why there I'd stand
Dead when they vanished with the sight of her).
And I saw that she had grown aware,
Queer puzzled face! of other things
Beyond the present and her own young speed,
Of yesterday and what new days might breed
Monstrously when the future brings
A charger with your late-lamented head:
Aware of other people's lives and will,
Aware, perhaps, aware even of me . . .
The joyous hope of it!   But still
I pitied her; for it was sad to see
A goddess shorn of her divinity.
In the midst of her speed she had made pause,
And doubts with all their threat of claws,

Outstripped till now by her unconsciousness,
Had seized on her; she was proved mortal now.
"Live, only live? For you were meant
Never to know a thought's distress,
But a long glad astonishment
At the world's beauty and your own.
The pity of you, goddess, grown
Perplexed and mortal!"
      Yet . . . yet . . . can it be
That she is aware, perhaps, even of me?

And life recedes, recedes; the curve is bare,
My handkerchief flutters blankly in the air;
And the question rumbles in the void:
Was she aware, was she after all aware?

MINOAN PORCELAIN

HER eyes of bright unwinking glaze
All imperturbable do not
Even make pretences to regard
The jutting absence of her stays,
Where many a Tyrian gallipot
Excites desire with spilth of nard.
The bistred rims above the fard
Of cheeks as red as bergamot
Attest that no shamefaced delays
Will clog fulfilment, nor retard
Full payment of the Cyprian's praise
Down to the last remorseful jot.
Hail priestess of we know not what
Strange cult of Mycenean days!

CRAPULOUS IMPRESSION

STILL life, still life . . . the high-lights shine
Hard and sharp on the bottles: the wine
Stands firmly solid in the glasses,
Smooth yellow ice, through which there passes
The lamp's bright pencil of down-struck light.
The fruits metallically gleam,
Globey in their heaped-up bowl,
And there are faces against the night
Of the outer room—faces that seem
Part of this still, still life . . . they've lost their soul.

And amongst these frozen faces you smiled,
Surprised, surprisingly, like a child:
And out of the frozen welter of sound
Your voice came quietly, quietly.
"What about God?" you said.   "I have found
Much to be said for Totality.
All, I take it, is God: God's all—
This bottle, for instance . . ."   I recall,
Dimly, that you took God by the neck—
God-in-the-bottle—and pushed Him across:
But I, without a moment's loss
Moved God-in-the-salt in front and shouted:
    "Check!"

COMPLAINT OF A POET MANQUÉ

WE judge by appearance merely:
If I can't think strangely, I can at least look queerly.

So I grew the hair so long on my head
That my mother wouldn't know me,
Till a woman in a night-club said,
As I was passing by,
"Hullo, here comes Salome."

I looked in the dirty gilt-edged glass,
And, oh Salome! there I was—
Positively jewelled, half a vampire,
With the soul in my eyes hanging dizzily
Like the gatherer of proverbial samphire
Over the brink of the crag of sense,
Looking down from perilous eminence
Into a gulf of windy night.
And there's straw in my tempestuous hair,
And I'm not a poet: but never despair!
I'll madly live the poems I shall never write.

SOCIAL AMENITIES

I AM getting on well with this anecdote,
When suddenly I recall
The many times I have told it of old,
And all the worked-up phrases, and the dying fall
Of voice, well timed in the crisis, the note
Of mock-heroic ingeniously struck—
The whole thing sticks in my throat,
And my face all tingles and pricks with shame
For myself and my hearers.
These are the social pleasures, my God!
But I finish the story triumphantly all the same.

TOPIARY

FAILING sometimes to understand
Why there are folk whose flesh should seem
Like carrion puffed with noisome steam,
Fly-blown to the eye that looks on it,
Fly-blown to the touch of a hand;
Why there are men without any legs,
Whizzing along on little trollies
With long long arms like apes':
Failing to see why God the Topiarist
Should train and carve and twist
Men's bodies into such fantastic shapes:
Yes, failing to see the point of it all, I sometimes wish
That I were a fabulous thing in a fool's mind,
Or, at the ocean bottom, in a world that is deaf and blind,
Very remote and happy, a great goggling fish.

ON THE 'BUS

SITTING on the top of the 'bus,
I bite my pipe and look at the sky.
Over my shoulder the smoke streams out
And my life with it.
"Conservation of energy," you say.
But I burn, I tell you, I burn;
And the smoke of me streams out
In a vanishing skein of grey.
Crash and bump . . . my poor bruised body!
I am a harp of twittering strings,
An elegant instrument, but infinitely second-hand,
And if I have not got phthisis it is only an accident.
Droll phenomena!

POINTS AND LINES

INSTANTS in the quiet, small sharp stars,
Pierce my spirit with a thrust whose speed
Baffles even the grasp of time.
Oh that I might reflect them
As swiftly, as keenly as they shine.
But I am a pool of waters, summer-still,
And the stars are mirrored across me;
Those stabbing points of the sky
Turned to a thread of shaken silver,
A long fine thread.

STANZAS

THOUGHT is an unseen net wherein our mind
Is taken and vainly struggles to be free:
Words, that should loose our spirit, do but bind
New fetters on our hoped-for liberty:
And action bears us onward like a stream
Past fabulous shores, scarce seen in our swift course;
Glorious—and yet its headlong currents seem
But backwaters of some diviner force.

There are slow curves, more subtle far than thought,
That stoop to carry the grace of a girl's breast;
And hanging flowers, so exquisitely wrought
In airy metal, that they seem possessed
Of souls; and there are distant hills that lift
The shoulder of a god towards the light;
And arrowy trees, sudden and sharp and swift,
Piercing the spirit deeply with delight.

B

Would I might make these miracles my own!
Like a pure angel, thinking colour and form;
Hardening to rage in a flame of chiselled stone;
Spilling my love like sunlight, golden and warm
On noonday flowers; speaking the song of birds
Among the branches; whispering the fall of rain;
Beyond all thought, past action and past words,
I would live in beauty, free from self and pain.

POEM

BOOKS and a coloured skein of thoughts were mine;
And magic words lay ripening in my soul
Till their much-whispered music turned a wine
Whose subtlest power was all in my control.

These things were mine, and they were real for me
As lips and darling eyes and a warm breast:
For I could love a phrase, a melody,
Like a fair woman, worshipped and possessed.

I scorned all fire that outward of the eyes
Could kindle passion; scorned, yet was afraid;
Feared, and yet envied those more deeply wise
Who saw the bright earth beckon and obeyed.

But a time came when, turning full of hate
And weariness from my remembered themes,
I wished my poet's pipe could modulate
Beauty more palpable than words and dreams.

All loveliness with which an act informs
The dim uncertain chaos of desire
Is mine to-day; it touches me, it warms
Body and spirit with its outward fire.

I am mine no more: I have become a part
Of that great earth that draws a breath and stirs
To meet the spring.   But I could wish my heart
Were still a winter of frosty gossamers.

SCENES OF THE MIND

I HAVE run where festival was loud
With drum and brass among the crowd
Of panic revellers, whose cries
Affront the quiet of the skies;
Whose dancing lights contract the deep
Infinity of night and sleep
To a narrow turmoil of troubled fire.
And I have found my heart's desire
In beechen caverns that autumn fills
With the blue shadowiness of distant hills;
Whose luminous grey pillars bear
The stooping sky: calm is the air,
Nor any sound is heard to mar
That crystal silence—as from far,
Far off a man may see
The busy world all utterly
Hushed as an old memorial scene.
Long evenings I have sat and been

Strangely content, while in my hands
I held a wealth of coloured strands,
Shimmering plaits of silk and skeins
Of soft bright wool.   Each colour drains
New life at the lamp's round pool of gold;
Each sinks again when I withhold
The quickening radiance, to a wan
And shadowy oblivion
Of what it was.   And in my mind
Beauty or sudden love has shined
And wakened colour in what was dead
And turned to gold the sullen lead
Of mean desires and everyday's
Poor thoughts and customary ways.
Sometimes in lands where mountains throw
Their silent spell on all below,
Drawing a magic circle wide
About their feet on every side,
Robbed of all speech and thought and act,
I have seen God in the cataract.
In falling water and in flame,
Never at rest, yet still the same,
God shows himself.   And I have known
The swift fire frozen into stone,
And water frozen changelessly
Into the death of gems.   And I
Long sitting by the thunderous mill
Have seen the headlong wheel made still,
And in the silence that ensued
Have known the endless solitude
Of being dead and utterly nought.
Inhabitant of mine own thought,

I look abroad, and all I see
Is my creation, made for me:
Along my thread of life are pearled
The moments that make up the world.

L'APRÈS-MIDI D'UN FAUNE

(From the French of Stéphane Mallarmé.)

I WOULD immortalize these nymphs: so bright
Their sunlit colouring, so airy light,
It floats like drowsy down.   Loved I a dream?
My doubts, born of oblivious darkness, seem
A subtle tracery of branches grown
The tree's true self—proving that I have known,
Thinking it love, the blushing of a rose.
But think. These nymphs, their loveliness ... suppose
They bodied forth your senses' fabulous thirst?
Illusion! which the blue eyes of the first,
As cold and chaste as is the weeping spring,
Beget: the other, sighing, passioning,
Is she the wind, warm in your fleece at noon?
No; through this quiet, when a weary swoon
Crushes and chokes the latest faint essay
Of morning, cool against the encroaching day,
There is no murmuring water, save the gush
Of my clear fluted notes; and in the hush
Blows never a wind, save that which through my reed
Puffs out before the rain of notes can speed
Upon the air, with that calm breath of art
That mounts the unwrinkled zenith visibly,
Where inspiration seeks its native sky.

You fringes of a calm Sicilian lake,
The sun's own mirror which I love to take,
Silent beneath your starry flowers, tell
How here I cut the hollow rushes, well
Tamed by my skill, when on the glaucous gold
Of distant lawns about their fountain cold
A living whiteness stirs like a lazy wave;
And at the first slow notes my panpipes gave
These flocking swans, these naiads, rather, fly
Or dive. Noon burns inert and tawny dry,
Nor marks how clean that Hymen slipped away
From me who seek in song the real A.
Wake, then, to the first ardour and the sight,
O lonely faun, of the old fierce white light,
With, lilies, one of you for innocence.
Other than their lips' delicate pretence,
The light caress that quiets treacherous lovers,
My breast, I know not how to tell, discovers
The bitten print of some immortal's kiss.
But hush! a mystery so great as this
I dare not tell, save to my double reed,
Which, sharer of my every joy and need,
Dreams down its cadenced monologues that we
Falsely confuse the beauties that we see
With the bright palpable shapes our song creates:
My flute, as loud as passion modulates,
Purges the common dream of flank and breast,
Seen through closed eyes and inwardly caressed,
Of every empty and monotonous line.

Bloom then, O Syrinx, in thy flight malign,
A reed once more beside our trysting-lake.

Proud of my music, let me often make
A song of goddesses and see their rape
Profanely done on many a painted shape.
So when the grape's transparent juice I drain,
I quell regret for pleasures past and feign
A new real grape. For holding towards the sky
The empty skin, I blow it tight and lie
Dream-drunk till evening, eyeing it.
                                         Tell o'er
Remembered joys and plump the grape once more.
Between the reeds I saw their bodies gleam
Who cool no mortal fever in the stream
Crying to the woods the rage of their desire:
And their bright hair went down in jewelled fire
Where crystal broke and dazzled shudderingly.
I check my swift pursuit: for see where lie,
Bruisèd, being twins in love, by languor sweet,
Two sleeping girls, clasped at my very feet.
I seize and run with them, nor part the pair,
Breaking this covert of frail petals, where
Roses drink scent of the sun and our light play
'Mid tumbled flowers shall match the death of day.
I love that virginal fury—ah, the wild
Thrill when a maiden body shrinks, defiled,
Shuddering like arctic light, from lips that sear
Its nakedness . . . the flesh in secret fear!
Contagiously through my linked pair it flies
Where innocence in either, struggling, dies,
Wet with fond tears or some less piteous dew.
Gay in the conquest of these fears, I grew
So rash that I must needs the sheaf divide
Of ruffled kisses heaven itself had tied.

For as I leaned to stifle in the hair
Of one my passionate laughter (taking care
With a stretched finger, that her innocence
Might stain with her companion's kindling sense
To touch the younger little one, who lay
Child-like unblushing) my ungrateful prey
Slips from me, freed by passion's sudden death
Nor heeds the frenzy of my sobbing breath.

Let it pass! others of their hair shall twist
A rope to drag me to those joys I missed.
See how the ripe pomegranates bursting red
To quench the thirst of the mumbling bees have
    bled;
So too our blood, kindled by some chance fire,
Flows for the swarming legions of desire.
At evening, when the woodland green turns gold
And ashen grey, 'mid the quenched leaves, behold!
Red Etna glows, by Venus visited,
Walking the lava with her snowy tread
Whene'er the flames in thunderous slumber die.
I hold the goddess!

                Ah, sure penalty!

By the unthinking soul and body swoon
At last beneath the heavy hush of noon.
Forgetful let me lie where summer's drouth
Sifts fine the sand and then with gaping mouth
Dream planet-struck by the grape's round wine-red
    star.

Nymphs, I shall see the shade that now you are.

MOLE

TUNNELLED in solid blackness creeps
The old mole-soul, and wakes or sleeps,
He knows not which, but tunnels on
Through ages of oblivion;
Until at last the long constraint
Of each hand-wall is lost, and faint
Comes daylight creeping from afar,
And mole-work grows crepuscular.
Tunnel meets air and bursts; mole sees
Men as strange as walking trees?
And far horizons smoking blue,
And chasing clouds for ever new;
Green hills, like lighted lamps aglow
Or quenched beneath the cloud-shadow;
Quenching and blazing turn by turn,
Spring's great green signals fitfully burn.
Mole travels on, but finds the steering
A harder task of pioneering
Than when he thridded through the strait
Blind catacombs that ancient fate
Had carved for him.   Stupid and dumb
And blind and touchless he had come
A way without a turn; but here,
Under the sky, the passenger

Chooses his own best way; and mole
Distracted wanders, yet his hole
Regrets not much wherein he crept,
But runs, a joyous nympholept,
This way and that, by all made mad—
River nymph and oread,
Ocean's daughters and Lorelei,
Combing the silken mystery,
The glaucous gold of her rivery tresses—
Each haunts the traveller, each possesses
The drunken wavering soul awhile;
Then with a phantom's cock-crow smile
Mocks craving with sheer vanishment.

   Mole-eyes grow hawk's: knowledge is lent
In grudging driblets that pay high
Unconscionable usury
To unrelenting life.   Mole learns
To travel more secure; the turns
Of his long way less puzzling seem,
And all those magic forms that gleam
In airy invitation cheat
Less often than they did of old.

   The earth slopes upward, fold by fold
Of quiet hills that meet the gold
Serenity of western skies.
Over the world's edge with clear eyes
Our mole transcendent sees his way
Tunnelled in light: he must obey
Necessity again and thrid

Close catacombs as erst he did,
Fate's tunnellings, himself must bore
Through the sunset's inmost core.
The guiding walls to each-hand shine
Luminous and crystalline;
And mole shall tunnel on and on,
Till night let fall oblivion.

TWO REALITIES

A WAGGON passed with scarlet wheels
    And a yellow body, shining new.
"Splendid!" said I. "How fine it feels
To be alive, when beauty peels
    The grimy husk from life." And you

Said, "Splendid!" and I thought you'd seen
    That waggon blazing down the street;
But I looked and saw that your gaze had been
On a child that was kicking an obscene
    Brown ordure with his feet.

Our souls are elephants, thought I,
    Remote behind a prisoning grill,
With trunks thrust out to peer and pry
And pounce upon reality;
    And each at his own sweet will

Seizes the bun that he likes best
And passes over all the rest.

PHILOSOPHY

"GOD needs no christening,"
  Pantheist mutters,
  "Love opens shutters
On heaven's glistening,
Flesh, key-hole listening,
  Hear what God utters" . . .
  Yes, but God stutters.

LEDA

LEDA

BROWN and bright as an agate, mountain-cool,
Eurotas singing slips from pool to pool;
Down rocky gullies; through the cavernous pines
And chestnut groves; down where the terraced vines
And gardens overhang; through valleys grey
With olive trees, into a soundless bay
Of the Ægean.   Silent and asleep
Lie those pools now: but where they dream most
      deep,
Men sometimes see ripples of shining hair
And the young grace of bodies pale and bare,
Shimmering far down—the ghosts these mirrors hold
Of all the beauty they beheld of old,
White limbs and heavenly eyes and the hair's river of
      gold,
For once these banks were peopled: Spartan girls
Loosed here their maiden girdles and their curls,
And stooping o'er the level water stole
His darling mirror from the sun through whole
Rapturous hours of gazing.
                                    The first star
Of all this milky constellation, far
Lovelier than any nymph of wood or green,
Was she whom Tyndarus had made his queen
For her sheer beauty and subtly moving grace—
Leda, the fairest of our mortal race.
Hymen had lit his torches but one week
About her bed (and still o'er her young cheek
Passed rosy shadows of those thoughts that sped
Across her mind, still virgin, still unwed,

For all her body was her own no more),
When Leda with her maidens to the shore
Of bright Eurotas came, to escape the heat
Of summer noon in waters coolly sweet.
By a brown pool which opened smooth and clear
Below the wrinkled water of a weir
They sat them down under an old fir-tree
To rest: and to the laughing melody
Of their sweet speech the river's rippling bore
A liquid burden, while the sun did pour
Pure colour out of heaven upon the earth.
The meadows seethed with the incessant mirth
Of grasshoppers, seen only when they flew
Their curves of scarlet or sudden dazzling blue.
Within the fir-tree's round of unpierced shade
The maidens sat with laughter and talk, or played,
Gravely intent, their game of knuckle-bones;
Or tossed from hand to hand the old dry cones
Littered about the tree.   And one did sing
A ballad of some far-off Spartan king,
Who took a wife, but left her, well-away!
Slain by his foes upon their wedding-day.
"That was a piteous story," Leda sighed,
"To be a widow ere she was a bride."
"Better," said one, "to live a virgin life
Alone, and never know the name of wife
And bear the ugly burden of a child
And have great pain by it.   Let me live wild,
A bird untamed by man!"   "Nay," cried another,
"I would be wife, if I should not be mother.
Cypris I honour; let the vulgar pay
Their gross vows to Lucina when they pray.

Our finer spirits would be blunted quite
By bestial teeming; but Love's rare delight
Wings the rapt soul towards Olympus' height."
"Delight?" cried Leda. "Love to me has brought
Nothing but pain and a world of shameful thought.
When they say love is sweet, the poets lie;
'Tis but a trick to catch poor maidens by.
What are their boasted pleasures? I am queen
To the most royal king the world has seen;
Therefore I should, if any woman might,
Know at its full that exquisite delight.
Yet these few days since I was made a wife
Have held more bitterness than all my life,
While I was yet a child." The great bright tears
Slipped through her lashes. "Oh, my childish
      years!
Years that were all my own, too sadly few,
When I was happy—and yet never knew
How happy till to-day!" Her maidens came
About her as she wept, whispering her name,
Leda, sweet Leda, with a hundred dear
Caressing words to soothe her heavy cheer.
At last she started up with a fierce pride
Upon her face. "I am a queen," she cried,
"But had forgotten it a while; and you,
Wenches of mine, you were forgetful too.
Undress me. We would bathe ourself." So proud
A queen she stood, that all her maidens bowed
In trembling fear and scarcely dared approach
To do her bidding. But at last the brooch
Pinned at her shoulder is undone, the wide
Girdle of silk beneath her breasts untied;

The tunic falls about her feet, and she
Steps from the crocus folds of drapery,
Dazzlingly naked, into the warm sun.
God-like she stood; then broke into a run,
Leaping and laughing in the light, as though
Life through her veins coursed with so swift a
     flow
Of generous blood and fire that to remain
Too long in statued queenliness were pain
To that quick soul, avid of speed and joy.
She ran, easily bounding, like a boy,
Narrow of haunch and slim and firm of breast.
Lovelier she seemed in motion than at rest,
If that might be, when she was never less,
Moving or still, than perfect loveliness.
At last, with cheeks afire and heaving flank,
She checked her race, and on the river's bank
Stood looking down at her own echoed shape
And at the fish that, aimlessly agape,
Hung midway up their heaven of flawless glass,
Like angels waiting for eternity to pass.
Leda drew breath and plunged; her gasping cry
Splashed up; the water circled brokenly
Out from that pearly shudder of dipped limbs;
The glittering pool laughed up its flowery brims,
And everything, save the poor fish, rejoiced:
Their idiot contemplation of the Moist,
The Cold, the Watery, was in a trice
Ended when Leda broke their crystal paradise.

Jove in his high Olympian chamber lay
Hugely supine, striving to charm away

C

In sleep the long, intolerable noon.
But heedless Morpheus still withheld his boon,
And Jove upon his silk-pavilioned bed
Tossed wrathful and awake.   His fevered head
Swarmed with a thousand fancies, which forecast
Delights to be, or savoured pleasures past.
Closing his eyes, he saw his eagle swift,
Headlong as his own thunder, stoop and lift
On pinions upward labouring the prize
Of beauty ravished for the envious skies.
He saw again that bright, adulterous pair,
Trapped by the limping husband unaware,
Fast in each other's arms, and faster in the snare—
And laughed remembering. Sometimes his thought
Went wandering over the earth and sought
Familiar places—temples by the sea,
Cities and islands; here a sacred tree
And there a cavern of shy nymphs.

                                    He rolled
About his bed, in many a rich fold
Crumpling his Babylonian coverlet,
And yawned and stretched.   The smell of his own
    sweat
Brought back to mind his Libyan desert-fane
Of mottled granite, with its endless train
Of pilgrim camels, reeking towards the sky
Ammonian incense to his hornéd deity;
The while their masters worshipped, offering
Huge teeth of ivory, while some would bring
Their Ethiop wives — sleek wineskins of black
    silk,
Jellied and huge from drinking asses' milk

Through years of tropical idleness, to pray
For offspring (whom he ever sent away
With prayers unanswered, lest their ebon race
Might breed and blacken the earth's comely face).
Noon pressed on him a hotter, heavier weight.
O Love in Idleness! how celibate
He felt! Libido like a nemesis
Scourged him with itching memories of bliss.
The satin of imagined skin was sleek
And supply warm against his lips and cheek,
And deep within soft hair's dishevelled dusk
His eyelids fluttered; like a flowery musk
The scent of a young body seemed to float
Faintly about him, close and yet remote—
For perfume and the essence of music dwell
In other worlds among the asphodel
Of unembodied life. Then all had flown;
His dream had melted. In his bed, alone,
Jove sweating lay and moaned, and longed in vain
To still the pulses of his burning pain.
In sheer despair at last he leapt from bed,
Opened the window and thrust forth his head
Into Olympian ether. One fierce frown
Rifted the clouds, and he was looking down
Into a gulf of azure calm; the rack
Seethed round about, tempestuously black;
But the god's eye could hold its angry thunders back.
There lay the world, down through the chasméd
        blue,
Stretched out from edge to edge unto his view;
And in the midst, bright as a summer's day
At breathless noon, the Mediterranean lay;

And Ocean round the world's dim fringes tossed
His glaucous waves in mist and distance lost;
And Pontus and the livid Caspian Sea
Stirred in their nightmare sleep uneasily.
And 'twixt the seas rolled the wide fertile land,
Dappled with green and tracts of tawny sand,
And rich, dark fallows and fields of flowers aglow
And the white, changeless silences of snow;
While here and there towns, like a living eye
Unclosed on earth's blind face, towards the sky
Glanced their bright conscious beauty.   Yet the sight
Of his fair earth gave him but small delight
Now in his restlessness: its beauty could
Do nought to quench the fever in his blood.
Desire lends sharpness to his searching eyes;
Over the world his focused passion flies
Quicker than chasing sunlight on a day
Of storm and golden April.   Far away
He sees the tranquil rivers of the East,
Mirrors of many a strange barbaric feast,
Where un-Hellenic dancing-girls contort
Their yellow limbs, and gibbering masks make sport
Under the moons of many-coloured light
That swing their lantern-fruitage in the night
Of overarching trees.   To him it seems
An alien world, peopled by insane dreams.
But these are nothing to the monstrous shapes—
Not men so much as bastardy of apes—
That meet his eyes in Africa.   Between
Leaves of grey fungoid pulp and poisonous green,
White eyes from black and browless faces stare.
Dryads with star-flowers in their woolly hair

Dance to the flaccid clapping of their own
Black dangling dugs through forests overgrown,
Platted with writhing creepers.   Horrified,
He sees them how they leap and dance, or glide,
Glimpse after black glimpse of a satin skin,
Among unthinkable flowers, to pause and grin
Out through a trellis of suppurating lips,
Of mottled tentacles barbed at the tips
And bloated hands and wattles and red lobes
Of pendulous gristle and enormous probes
Of pink and slashed and tasselled flesh . . .

                                        He turns
Northward his sickened sight.   The desert burns
All life away.   Here in the forkéd shade
Of twin-humped towering dromedaries laid,
A few gaunt folk are sleeping: fierce they seem
Even in sleep, and restless as they dream.
He would be fearful of a desert bride
As of a brown asp at his sleeping side,
Fearful of her white teeth and cunning arts.
Further, yet further, to the ultimate parts
Of the wide earth he looks, where Britons go
Painted among their swamps, and through the snow
Huge hairy snuffling beasts pursue their prey—
Fierce men, as hairy and as huge as they.

Bewildered furrows deepen the Thunderer's scowl;
This world so vast, so variously foul—
Who can have made its ugliness?   In what
Revolting fancy were the Forms begot
Of all these monsters?   What strange deity—
So barbarously not a Greek!—was he

Who could mismake such beings in his own
Distorted image.   Nay, the Greeks alone
Were men; in Greece alone were bodies fair,
Minds comely.   In that all-but-island there,
Cleaving the blue sea with its promontories,
Lies the world's hope, the seed of all the glories
That are to be; there, too, must surely live
She who alone can medicinably give
Ease with her beauty to the Thunderer's pain.
Downwards he bends his fiery eyes again,
Glaring on Hellas.   Like a beam of light,
His intent glances touch the mountain height
With passing flame and probe the valleys deep,
Rift the dense forest and the age-old sleep
Of vaulted antres on whose pebbly floor
Gallop the loud-hoofed Centaurs; and the roar
Of more than human shouting underground
Pulses in living palpable waves of sound
From wall to wall, until it rumbles out
Into the air; and at that hollow shout
That seems an utterance of the whole vast hill,
The shepherds cease their laughter and are still.
Cities asleep under the noonday sky
Stir at the passage of his burning eye;
And in their huts the startled peasants blink
At the swift flash that bursts through every chink
Of wattled walls, hearkening in fearful wonder
Through lengthened seconds for the crash of thunder—
Which follows not: they are the more afraid.
Jove seeks amain.   Many a country maid,
Whose sandalled feet pass down familiar ways
Among the olives, but whose spirit strays

Through lovelier lands of fancy, suddenly
Starts broad awake out of her dream to see
A light that is not of the sun, a light
Darted by living eyes, consciously bright;
She sees and feels it like a subtle flame
Mantling her limbs with fear and maiden shame
And strange desire. Longing and terrified,
She hides her face, like a new-wedded bride
Who feels rough hands that seize and hold her fast;
And swooning falls. The terrible light has passed;
She wakes; the sun still shines, the olive trees
Tremble to whispering silver in the breeze
And all is as it was, save she alone
In whose dazed eyes this deathless light has shone:
For never, never from this day forth will she
In earth's poor passion find felicity,
Or love of mortal man. A god's desire
Has seared her soul; nought but the same strong fire
Can kindle the dead ash to life again,
And all her years will be a lonely pain.

Many a thousand had he looked upon,
Thousands of mortals, young and old; but none—
Virgin, or young ephebus, or the flower
Of womanhood culled in its full-blown hour—
Could please the Thunderer's sight or touch his
    mind;
The longed-for loveliness was yet to find.
Had beauty fled, and was there nothing fair
Under the moon? The fury of despair
Raged in the breast of heaven's Almighty Lord;
He gnashed his foamy teeth and rolled and roared

In bull-like agony.   Then a great calm
Descended on him: cool and healing balm
Touched his immortal fury.   He had spied
Young Leda where she stood, poised on the river-
        side.

Even as she broke the river's smooth expanse,
Leda was conscious of that hungry glance,
And knew it for an eye of fearful power
That did so hot and thunderously lour,
She knew not whence, on her frail nakedness.
Jove's heart held but one thought: he must possess
That perfect form or die—possess or die.
Unheeded prayers and supplications fly,
Thick as a flock of birds, about his ears,
And smoke of incense rises; but he hears
Nought but the soft falls of that melody
Which is the speech of Leda; he can see
Nought but that almost spiritual grace
Which is her body, and that heavenly face
Where gay, sweet thoughts shine through, and eyes
        are bright
With purity and the soul's inward light.
Have her he must: the teasel-fingered burr
Sticks not so fast in a wild beast's tangled fur
As that insistent longing in the soul
Of mighty Jove. Gods, men, earth, heaven, the whole
Vast universe was blotted from his thought
And nought remained but Leda's laughter, nought
But Leda's eyes.   Magnified by his lust,
She was the whole world now; have her he must, he
        must . . .

His spirit worked; how should he gain his end
With most deliciousness?   What better friend,
What counsellor more subtle could he find
Than lovely Aphrodite, ever kind .
To hapless lovers, ever cunning, too,
In all the tortuous ways of love to do
And plan the best?   To Paphos then!   His will
And act were one; and straight, invisible,
He stood in Paphos, breathing the languid air
By Aphrodite's couch.   O heavenly fair
She was, and smooth and marvellously young!
On Tyrian silk she lay, and purple hung
About her bed in folds of fluted light
And shadow, dark as wine.   Two doves, more
      white
Even than the white hand on the purple lying
Like a pale flower wearily dropped, were flying
With wings that made an odoriferous stir,
Dropping faint dews of bakkaris and myrrh,
Musk and the soul of sweet flowers cunningly
Ravished from transient petals as they die.
Two stripling cupids on her either hand
Stood near with winnowing plumes and gently
      fanned
Her hot, love-fevered cheeks and eyelids burning.
Another, crouched at the bed's foot, was turning
A mass of scattered parchments—vows or plaints
Or glad triumphant thanks which Venus' saints,
Martyrs and heroes, on her altars strewed
With bitterest tears or gifts of gratitude.
From the pile heaped at Aphrodite's feet
The boy would take a leaf, and in his sweet,

Clear voice would read what mortal tongues can tell
In stammering verse of those ineffable
Pleasures and pains of love, heaven and uttermost hell.
Jove hidden stood and heard him read these lines
Of votive thanks—

>Cypris, this little silver lamp to thee
>>I dedicate.
>It was my fellow-watcher, shared with me
>Those swift, short hours, when raised above my fate
>In Sphenura's white arms I drank
>>Of immortality.

"A pretty lamp, and I will have it placed
Beside the narrow bed of some too chaste
Sister of virgin Artemis, to be
A night-long witness of her cruelty.
Read me another, boy," and Venus bent
Her ear to listen to this short lament.

>Cypris, Cypris, I am betrayed!
>Under the same wide mantle laid
>I found them, faithless, shameless pair!
>Making love with tangled hair.

"Alas," the goddess cried, "nor god, nor man,
Nor medicinable balm, nor magic can
Cast out the demon jealousy, whose breath
Withers the rose of life, save only time and death."
Another sheet he took and read again.

>Farewell to love, and hail the long, slow pain
>Of memory that backward turns to joy.
>O I have danced enough and enough sung;
>My feet shall be still now and my voice mute;
>Thine are these withered wreaths, this Lydian flute,
>>Cypris; I once was young.

And piêtous Aphrodite wept to think
How fadingly upon death's very brink
Beauty and love take hands for one short kiss—
And then the wreaths are dust, the bright-eyed
    bliss
Perished, and the flute still. "Read on, read on."
But ere the page could start, a lightning shone
Suddenly through the room, and they were 'ware
Of some great terrible presence looming there.
And it took shape—huge limbs, whose every line
A symbol was of power and strength divine,
And it was Jove.
                    "Daughter, I come," said he,
"For counsel in a case that touches me
Close, to the very life."   And he straightway
Told her of all his restlessness that day
And of his sight of Leda, and how great
Was his desire.   And so in close debate
Sat the two gods, planning their rape; while she,
Who was to be their victim, joyously
Laughed like a child in the sudden breathless chill
And splashed and swam, forgetting every ill
And every fear and all, save only this:
That she was young, and it was perfect bliss
To be alive where suns so goldenly shine,
And bees go drunk with fragrant honey-wine,
And the cicadas sing from morn till night,
And rivers run so cool and pure and bright . . .
Stretched all her length, arms under head, she lay
In the deep grass, while the sun kissed away
The drops that sleeked her skin.   Slender and fine
As those old images of the gods that shine

With smooth-worn silver, polished through the
    years
By the touching lips of countless worshippers,
Her body was; and the sun's golden heat
Clothed her in softest flame from head to feet
And was her mantle, that she scarcely knew
The conscious sense of nakedness.   The blue,
Far hills and the faint fringes of the sky
Shimmered and pulsed in the heat uneasily,
And hidden in the grass, cicadas shrill
Dizzied the air with ceaseless noise, until
A listener might wonder if they cried
In his own head or in the world outside.
Sometimes she shut her eyelids, and wrapped
    round
In a red darkness, with the muffled sound
And throb of blood beating within her brain,
Savoured intensely to the verge of pain
Her own young life, hoarded it up behind
Her shuttered lids, until, too long confined,
It burst them open and her prisoned soul
Flew forth and took possession of the whole
Exquisite world about her and was made
A part of it.   Meanwhile her maidens played,
Singing an ancient song of death and birth,
Seed-time and harvest, old as the grey earth,
And moving to their music in a dance
As immemorial.   A numbing trance
Came gradually over her, as though
Flake after downy-feathered flake of snow
Had muffled all her senses, drifting deep
And warm and quiet.

From this all-but sleep
She started into life again; the sky
Was full of a strange tumult suddenly—
Beating of mighty wings and shrill-voiced fear
And the hoarse scream of rapine following near.
In the high windlessness above her flew,
Dazzlingly white on the untroubled blue,
A splendid swan, with outstretched neck and wing
Spread fathom wide, and closely following
An eagle, tawny and black.   This god-like pair
Circled and swooped through the calm of upper air,
The eagle striking and the white swan still
'Scaping as though by happy miracle
The imminent talons.   For the twentieth time
The furious hunter stooped, to miss and climb
A mounting spiral into the height again.
He hung there poised, eyeing the grassy plain
Far, far beneath, where the girls' upturned faces
Were like white flowers that bloom in open places
Among the scarcely budded woods.   And they
Breathlessly watched and waited; long he lay,
Becalmed upon that tideless sea of light,
While the great swan with slow and creaking flight
Went slanting down towards safety, where the stream
Shines through the trees below, with glance and
    gleam
Of blue aerial eyes that seem to give
Sense to the sightless earth and make it live.
The ponderous wings beat on and no pursuit:
Stiff as the painted kite that guards the fruit,
Afloat o'er orchards ripe, the eagle yet
Hung as at anchor, seeming to forget

His uncaught prey, his rage unsatisfied.
Still, quiet, dead . . . and then the quickest-eyed
Had lost him. Like a star unsphered, a stone
Dropped from the vault of heaven, a javelin thrown,
He swooped upon his prey. Down, down he came,
And through his plumes with a noise of wind-blown
    flame
Loud roared the air. From Leda's lips a cry
Broke, and she hid her face—she could not see him
    die,
Her lovely, hapless swan.
                Ah, had she heard,
Even as the eagle hurtled past, the word
That treacherous pair exchanged. "Peace," cried
    the swan;
"Peace, daughter. All my strength will soon be
    gone,
Wasted in tedious flying, ere I come
Where my desire hath set its only home."
"Go," said the eagle, "I have played my part,
Roused pity for your plight in Leda's heart
(Pity the mother of voluptuousness).
Go, father Jove; be happy; for success
Attends this moment."
              On the queen's numbed sense
Fell a glad shout that ended sick suspense,
Bidding her lift once more towards the light
Her eyes, by pity closed against a sight
Of blood and death—her eyes, how happy now
To see the swan still safe, while far below,
Brought by the force of his eluded stroke
So near to earth that with his wings he woke

A gust whose sudden silvery motion stirred
The meadow grass, struggled the sombre bird
Of rage and rapine.   Loud his scream and hoarse
With baffled fury as he urged his course
Upwards again on threshing pinions wide.
But the fair swan, not daring to abide
This last assault, dropped with the speed of fear
Towards the river.   Like a winged spear,
Outstretching his long neck, rigid and straight,
Aimed at where Leda on the bank did wait
With open arms and kind, uplifted eyes
And voice of tender pity, down he flies.
Nearer, nearer, terribly swift, he sped
Directly at the queen; then widely spread
Resisting wings, and breaking his descent
'Gainst his own wind, all speed and fury spent,
The great swan fluttered slowly down to rest
And sweet security on Leda's breast.
Menacingly the eagle wheeled above her;
But Leda, like a noble-hearted lover
Keeping his child-beloved from tyrannous harm,
Stood o'er the swan and, with one slender arm
Imperiously lifted, waved away
The savage foe, still hungry for his prey.
Baffled at last, he mounted out of sight
And the sky was void—save for a single white
Swan's feather moulted from a harassed wing
That down, down, with a rhythmic balancing
From side to side dropped sleeping on the air.
Down, slowly down over that dazzling pair,
Whose different grace in union was a birth
Of unimagined beauty on the earth:

So lovely that the maidens standing round
Dared scarcely look. Couched on the flowery
    ground
Young Leda lay, and to her side did press
The swan's proud-arching opulent loveliness,
Stroking the snow-soft plumage of his breast
With fingers slowly drawn, themselves caressed
By the warm softness where they lingered, loth
To break away. Sometimes against their growth
Ruffling the feathers inlaid like little scales
On his sleek neck, the pointed finger-nails
Rasped on the warm, dry, puckered skin beneath;
And feeling it she shuddered, and her teeth
Grated on edge; for there was something strange
And snake-like in the touch. He, in exchange,
Gave back to her, stretching his eager neck,
For every kiss a little amorous peck;
Rubbing his silver head on her gold tresses,
And with the nip of horny dry caresses
Leaving upon her young white breast and cheek
And arms the red print of his playful beak.
Closer he nestled, mingling with the slim
Austerity of virginal flank and limb
His curved and florid beauty, till she felt
That downy warmth strike through her flesh and
    melt
The bones and marrow of her strength away.
One lifted arm bent o'er her brow, she lay
With limbs relaxed, scarce breathing, deathly still;
Save when a quick, involuntary thrill
Shook her sometimes with passing shudderings,
As though some hand had plucked the aching strings

Of life itself, tense with expectancy.
And over her the swan shook slowly free
The folded glory of his wings, and made
A white-walled tent of soft and luminous shade
To be her veil and keep her from the shame
Of naked light and the sun's noonday flame.

Hushed lay the earth and the wide, careless sky.
Then one sharp sound, that might have been a cry
Of utmost pleasure or of utmost pain,
Broke sobbing forth, and all was still again.

THE BIRTH OF GOD

NIGHT is a void about me; I lie alone;
And water drips, like an idiot clicking his tongue,
Senselessly, ceaselessly, endlessly drips
Into the waiting silence, grown
Emptier for this small inhuman sound.
My love is gone, my love who is tender and young.
O smooth warm body! O passionate lips!
I have stretched forth hands in the dark and nothing
          found:
The silence is huge as the sky—I lie alone—
My narrow room, a darkness that knows no bound.

How shall I fill this measureless
Deep void that the taking away
Of a child's slim beauty has made?

D

Slender she is and small, but the loneliness
She has left is a night no stars allay,
And I am cold and afraid.

Long, long ago, cut off from the wolfish pack,
From the warm, immediate touch of friends and
    mate,
Lost and alone, alone in the utter black
Of a forest night, some far-off, beast-like man,
Cowed by the cold indifferent hate
Of the northern silence, crouched in fear,
When through his bleared and suffering mind
A sudden tremor of comfort ran,
And the void was filled by a rushing wind,
And he breathed a sense of something friendly and
    near,
And in privation the life of God began.

Love, from your loss shall a god be born to fill
The emptiness, where once you were,
With friendly knowledge and more than a lover's
    will
To ease despair?
Shall I feed longing with what it hungers after,
Seeing in earth and sea and air
A lover's smiles, hearing a lover's laughter,
Feeling love everywhere?

The night drags on.   Darkness and silence grow,
And with them my desire has grown,
My bitter need.   Alas, I know,
I know that here I lie alone.

ON HAMPSTEAD HEATH

BENEATH the sunlight and blue of all-but Autumn
  The grass sleeps goldenly: woodland and distant
    hill
Shine through the gauzy air in a dust of golden
    pollen,
  And even the glittering leaves are almost still.

Scattered on the grass, like a ragman's bundles care-
    lessly dropped,
  Men sleep outstretched or, sprawling, bask in the
    sun;
Here glows a woman's bright dress and here a child
    is sitting,
  And I lie down and am one of the sleepers, one

Like the rest of this tumbled crowd.   Do they all, I
    wonder,
  Feel anguish grow with the calm day's slow decline,
Longing, as I, for a shattering wind, a passion
  Of bodily pain to be the soul's anodyne?

SYMPATHY

THE irony of being two . . .!
Grey eyes, wide open suddenly,
Regard me and enquire; I see a face
Grave and unquiet in tenderness.

Heart-rending question of women—never answered:
"Tell me, tell me, what are you thinking of?"
Oh, the pain and foolishness of love!
What can I do but make my old grimace,
Ending it with a kiss, as I always do?

MALE AND FEMALE CREATED HE THEM

DIAPHENIA, drunk with sleep,
Drunk with pleasure, drunk with fatigue,
Feels her Corydon's fingers creep—
Ring-finger, middle finger, index, thumb—
Strummingly over the smooth sleek drum
Of her thorax.

             Meanwhile Händel's Gigue
Turns in Corydon's absent mind
To Yakka-Hoola.

          She can find
No difference in the thrilling touch
Of one who, now, in everything
Is God-like.   "Was there ever such
Passion as ours?"

            His pianoing
Gives place to simple arithmetic's
Simplest constatations:—six
Letters in Gneiss and three in Gnu:
Luncheon to-day cost three and two;
In a year—he couldn't calculate
Three-sixty-five times thirty-eight,

Figuring with printless fingers on
Her living parchment.

                "Corydon!
I faint, faint, faint at your dear touch.
Say, is it possible . . . to love too much?"

FROM THE PILLAR

SIMEON, the withered stylite,
    Sat gloomily looking down
Upon each roof and skylight
    In all the seething town.

And in every upper chamber,
    On roofs, where the orange flowers
Make weary men remember
    The perfume of long-dead hours,

He saw the wine-drenched riot
    Of harlots and human beasts,
And how celestial quiet
    Was shattered by their feasts.

The steam of fetid vices
    From a thousand lupanars,
Like smoke of sacrifices,
    Reeked up to the heedless stars.

And the saint from his high fastness
    Of purity apart
Cursed them and their unchasteness,
    And envied them in his heart.

JONAH

A CREAM of phosphorescent light
Floats on the wash that to and fro
Slides round his feet—enough to show
Many a pendulous stalactite
Of naked mucus, whorls and wreaths
And huge festoons of mottled tripes
And smaller palpitating pipes
Through which a yeasty liquor seethes.

Seated upon the convex mound
Of one vast kidney, Jonah prays
And sings his canticles and hymns,
Making the hollow vault resound
God's goodness and mysterious ways,
Till the great fish spouts music as he swims.

VARIATIONS ON A THEME

SWAN, Swan,
Yesterday you were
The whitest of things in this dark winter.
To-day the snow has made of your plumes
An unwashed pocket handkercher,
An unwashed pocket handkercher . . .
"Lancashire, to Lancashire!"—
Tune of the antique trains long ago:
Each summer holiday a milestone
Backwards, backwards:—
Tenby, Barmouth, and year by year.

All the different hues of the sea,
Blue, green and blue.
But on this river of muddy jade
There swims a yellow swan,
And along the bank the snow lies dazzlingly white.

A MELODY BY SCARLATTI

How clear under the trees,
How softly the music flows,
Rippling from one still pool to another
Into the lake of silence.

A SUNSET

OVER against the triumph and the close—
  Amber and green and rose—
    Of this short day,
The pale ghost of the moon grows living-bright
  Once more, as the last light
    Ebbs slowly away.
Darkening the fringes of these western glories
  The black phantasmagories
    Of cloud advance
With noiseless footing—vague and villainous shapes,
  Wrapped in their ragged fustian capes,
    Of some grotesque romance.
But overhead where, like a pool between
  Dark rocks, the sky is green
    And clear and deep,

Floats windlessly a cloud, with curving breast
    Flushed by the fiery west,
        In god-like sleep . . .
And in my mind opens a sudden door
    That lets me see once more
        A little room
With night beyond the window, chill and damp,
    And one green-lighted lamp
        Tempering the gloom,
While here within, close to me, touching me
    (Even the memory
        Of my desire
Shakes me like fear), you sit with scattered hair;
    And all your body bare
        Before the fire
Is lapped about with rosy flame. . . . But still,
    Here on the lonely hill,
        I walk alone;
Silvery green is the moon's lamp overhead,
    The cloud sleeps warm and red,
        And you are gone.

LIFE AND ART

YOU have sweet flowers for your pleasure,
    You laugh with the bountiful earth
In its richness of summer treasure:
    Where now are your flowers and your mirth?
Petals and cadenced laughter,
    Each in a dying fall,
Droop out of life; and after
    Is nothing; they were all.

But we from the death of roses
   That three suns perfume and gild
With a kiss, till the fourth discloses
   A withered wreath, have distilled
The fullness of one rare phial,
   Whose nimble life shall outrun
The circling shadow on the dial,
   Outlast the tyrannous sun.

FIRST PHILOSOPHER'S SONG

A POOR degenerate from the ape,
Whose hands are four, whose tail's a limb,
I contemplate my flaccid shape
And know I may not rival him,

Save with my mind—a nimbler beast
Possessing a thousand sinewy tails,
A thousand hands, with which it scales,
Greedy of luscious truth, the greased

Poles and the coco palms of thought,
Thrids easily through the mangrove maze
Of metaphysics, walks the taut
Frail dangerous liana ways

That link across wild gulfs remote
Analogies between tree and tree;
Outruns the hare, outhops the goat;
Mind fabulous, mind sublime and free!

But oh, the sound of simian mirth!
Mind, issued from the monkey's womb,
Is still umbilical to earth,
Earth its home and earth its tomb.

SECOND PHILOSOPHER'S SONG

IF, O my Lesbia, I should commit,
Not fornication, dear, but suicide,
My Thames-blown body (Pliny vouches it)
Would drift face upwards on the oily tide
With the other garbage, till it putrefied.

But you, if all your lovers' frozen hearts
Conspired to send you, desperate, to drown—
Your maiden modesty would float face down,
And men would weep upon your hinder parts.

'Tis the Lord's doing.   Marvellous is the plan
By which this best of worlds is wisely planned.
One law He made for woman, one for man:
We bow the head and do not understand.

FIFTH PHILOSOPHER'S SONG

A MILLION million spermatozoa,
    All of them alive:
Out of their cataclysm but one poor Noah
    Dare hope to survive.

And among that million minus one
    Might have chanced to be
Shakespeare, another Newton, a new Donne—
    But the One was Me.

Shame to have ousted your betters thus,
    Taking ark while the others remained outside!
Better for all of us, froward Homunculus,
    If you'd quietly died!

NINTH PHILOSOPHER'S SONG

GOD'S in His Heaven: He never issues
    (Wise Man!) to visit this world of ours.
Unchecked the cancer gnaws our tissues,
    Stops to lick chops and then again devours.

Those find, who most delight to roam
    'Mid castles of remotest Spain,
That there's, thank Heaven, no place like home;
    So they set out upon their travels again.

Beauty for some provides escape,
    Who gain a happiness in eyeing
The gorgeous buttocks of the ape
    Or Autumn sunsets exquisitely dying.

And some to better worlds than this
    Mount up on wings as frail and misty
As passion's all-too-transient kiss
    (Though afterwards—oh, *omne animal triste*!)

But I, too rational by half
   To live but where I bodily am,
Can only do my best to laugh,
   Can only sip my misery dram by dram.

While happier mortals take to drink,
   A dolorous dipsomaniac,
Fuddled with grief I sit and think,
   Looking upon the bile when it is black.

Then brim the bowl with atrabilious liquor!
   We'll pledge our Empire vast across the flood:
For Blood, as all men know, than Water's thicker,
   But water's wider, thank the Lord, than Blood.

MORNING SCENE

LIGHT through the latticed blind
Spans the dim intermediate space
With parallels of luminous dust
To gild a nuptial couch, where Goya's mind
Conceived those agonising hands, that hair
Scattered, and half a sunlit bosom bare,
And, imminently above them, a red face
Fixed in the imbecile earnestness of lust.

VERREY'S

HERE, every winter's night at eight,
Epicurus lies in state,
Two candles at his head and two
Candles at his feet.   A few

Choice spirits watch beneath the vault
Of his dim chapel, where default
Of music fills the pregnant air
With subtler requiem and prayer
Than ever an organ wrought with notes
Spouted from its tubal throats.
Black Ethiopia's Holy Child,
The Cradled Bottle, breathes its mild
Meek spirit on the ravished nose,
The palate and the tongue of those
Who piously partake with me
Of this funereal agape.

FRASCATI'S

BUBBLE-BREASTED swells the dome
Of this my spiritual home,
From whose nave the chandelier,
Schaffhausen frozen, tumbles sheer.
We in the round balcony sit,
Lean o'er and look into the pit
Where feed the human bears beneath,
Champing with their gilded teeth.
What negroid holiday makes free
With such priapic revelry?
What songs?   What gongs?   What nameless
      rites?
What gods like wooden stalagmites?
What steam of blood or kidney pie?
What blasts of Bantu melody?

Ragtime. . . . But when the wearied Band
Swoons to a waltz, I take her hand,
And there we sit in blissful calm,
Quietly sweating palm to palm.

FATIGUE

THE mind has lost its Aristotelian elegance of shape:
there is only a darkness where bubbles and inconse-
quent balloons float up to burst their luminous cheeks
and vanish.

A woman with a basket on her head: a Chinese
lantern quite askew: the vague bright bulging of
chemists' window bottles; and then in my ears the
distant noise of a great river of people. And phrases,
phrases—

It is only a question of saddle-bags,
Stane Street and Gondibert,
Foals in Iceland (or was it Foals in aspic?).

As that small reddish devil turns away with an
insolent jut of his hindquarters, I become aware that
his curling pug's tail is an electric bell-push. But
that does not disquiet me so much as the sight of all
these polished statues twinkling with high lights and
all of them grotesque and all of them colossal.

THE MERRY-GO-ROUND

THE machine is ready to start. The symbolic beasts
grow resty, curveting where they stand at their places
in the great blue circle of the year. The Showman's

voice rings out. "Montez, mesdames et messieurs, montez. You, sir, must bestride the Ram. You will take the Scorpion. Yours, madame, is the Goat. As for you there, blackguard boy, you must be content with the Fishes. I have allotted you the Virgin, mademoiselle." . . . "Polisson!" "Pardon, pardon. Evidemment, c'est le Sagittaire qu'on demande. Ohé, les dards! The rest must take what comes. The Twins shall counterpoise one another in the Scales. So, so. Now away we go, away."

Ha, what keen air. Wind of the upper spaces. Snuff it deep, drink in the intoxication of our speed. Hark how the music swells and rings . . . sphery music, music of every vagabond planet, every rooted star; sound of winds and seas and all the simmering millions of life. Moving, singing . . . so with a roar and a rush round we go and round, for ever whirling on a ceaseless Bank Holiday of drunken life and speed.

But I happened to look inwards among the machinery of our roundabout, and there I saw a slobbering cretin grinding at a wheel and sweating as he ground, and grinding eternally. And when I perceived that he was the author of all our speed and that the music was of his making, that everything depended on his grinding wheel, I thought I would like to get off. But we were going too fast.

BACK STREETS

BACK streets, gutters of stagnating darkness where men breathe something that is not so much air as a kind of rarefied slime. . . . I look back down the tunnelled darkness of a drain to where, at the mouth, a broader, windier water-way glitters with the gay speed and motion of sunlit life. But around all is dimly rotting; and the inhabitants are those squamous, phosphorescent creatures that darkness and decay beget. Little men, sheathed tightly in clothes of an exaggeratedly fashionable cheapness, hurry along the pavements, jaunty and at the same time furtive. There is a thin layer of slime over all of them. And then there are the eyes of the women, with their hard glitter that is only of the surface. They see acutely, but in a glassy, superficial way, taking in the objects round them no more than my western windows retain the imprint of the sunset that enriches them.

Back streets, exhalations of a difficult puberty, I once lived on the fringes of them.

LAST THINGS

THERE have been visions, dark in the minds of men, death and corruption dancing across the secular abyss that separates eternity from time to where sits the ineluctable judge, waiting, waiting through the ages, and ponders all his predestinated decrees. There will be judgment, and each, in an agony of shame, reluctant yet compelled, will turn his own accuser. For

> Tunc tua gesta noxia
> Secreta quoque turpia
> Videbunt mille millia
> Virorum circumstantia.

There under the unwinking gaze of all the legions of just men made perfect, the poor prisoner will uncover each dirty secret of his heart, will act over again each shameful scene of his life. And those eyes of saints and angels will shine impassively down upon his beastliness, and to him, as he looks at their steady brilliance, they will seem a million of little blazing loopholes slotted in the walls of hell.

Hildebert, this was your vision as you brooded over death and judgment, hell and heaven, in your cloister, a thousand years ago. Do you not envy us our peace of mind who know not four ultimates, but only one? For whom the first of the Last Things is also the last —us, whom death annihilates with all our shame and all our folly, leaving no trace behind.

GOTHIC

SHARP spires pierce upwards, and the clouds are full of tumbling bells. Reckless, breakneck, head over heels down an airy spiral of stairs run the bells. "Upon Paul's steeple stands a tree."

Up again and then once more to the bottom, two steps at a time. "As full of apples as can be."

Up again and down again: centuries of climbing have not worn the crystal smoothness of the degrees.

Along the bellying clouds the little boys of London Town come running, running as best they may, seeing that at every step they sink ankle-deep through

E

the woolly surface into the black heart of thunder
beneath.

The apples on the trees are swaying in the wind,
rocking to the clamour of bells. The leaves are of
bright green copper, and rattle together with a scaly
sound. At the roots of the tree sit four gargoyles
playing a little serious game with dice. The hunch-
backed ape has won from the manticore that crooked
French crown with a hole in it which the manticore
got from the friar with the strawberry nose; he had
it in turn as an alms from the grave knight who lies
with crossed legs down there, through the clouds and
the dizzy mist of bell-ringing, where the great church
is a hollow ship, full of bright candles, and stable in
the midst of dark tempestuous seas.

EVENING PARTY

"SANS Espoir, sans Espoir . . ." sang the lady
while the piano laboriously opened its box of old
sardines in treacle. One detected ptomaine in the
syrup.

Sans Espoir . . . I thought of the rhymes—soir,
nonchaloir, reposoir—the dying falls of a symbolism
grown sadly suicidal before the broad Flemish back
of the singer, the dewlaps of her audience. Sans
Espoir. The listeners wore the frozen rapture of
those who gaze upon the uplifted Host.

Catching one another's eye, we had a simultaneous
vision of pews, of hyenas and hysteria.

Three candles were burning. They behaved like English aristocrats in a French novel—perfectly, impassively. I tried to imitate their milordliness.

One of the candles flickered, snickered. Was it a draught or was it laughter?

Flickering, snickering—candles, you betrayed me. I had to laugh too.

BEAUTY

I

THERE is a sea somewhere—whether in the lampless crypts of the earth, or among sunlit islands, or that which is an unfathomable and terrifying question between the archipelagos of stars—there is a sea (and perhaps its tides have filled those green transparent pools that glint like eyes in a spring storm-cloud) which is for ever troubled and in travail—a bubbling and a heaving up of waters as though for the birth of a fountain.

The sick and the crippled lie along the brims in expectation of the miracle. And at last, at last . . .

A funnel of white water is twisted up and so stands, straight and still by the very speed of its motion.

It drinks the light; slowly it is infused with colour, rose and mother-of-pearl. Slowly it takes shape, a heavenly body.

O dazzling Anadyomene!

The flakes of foam break into white birds about her head, fall again in a soft avalanche of flowers. Perpetual miracle, beauty endlessly born.

II

STEAMERS, in all your travelling have you trailed the meshes of your long expiring white nets across this sea, or dipped in it your sliding rail, or balanced your shadow far far down upon its glass-green sand? Or, forgetting the preoccupations of commerce and the well-oiled predestination of your machinery, did you ever put in at the real Paphos?

III

IN the city of Troy, whither our Argonautical voyages had carried us, we found Helen and that lamentable Cressid who was to Chaucer the feminine paradox, untenably fantastic but so devastatingly actual, the crystal ideal—flawed; and to Shakespeare the inevitable trull, flayed to show her physiological machinery and the logical conclusion of even the most heart-rendingly ingenuous gesture of maidenhood. (But, bless you! our gorge doesn't rise. We are cynically well up in the damning Theory of woman, which makes it all the more amusing to watch ourselves in the ecstatic practice of her. Unforeseen perversity.)

Fabulous Helen! At her firm breasts they used to mould delicate drinking cups which made the sourest vinegar richly poisonous.

The geometry of her body had utterly outwitted Euclid, and the Philosophers were baffled by curves of a subtlety infinitely more elusive and Eleusinian than the most oracular speculations of Parmenides.

They did their best to make a coherent system out of the incompatible, but empirically established, facts of her. Time, for instance, was abolished within the circle of her arms. "It is eternity when her lips touch me," Paris had remarked. And yet this same Paris was manifestly and notoriously falling into a decline, had lost whatever sense or beauty he once possessed, together with his memory and all skill in the nine arts which are memory's daughters. How was it then, these perplexed philosophers wondered, that she could at one and the same moment give eternity like a goddess, while she was vampiring away with that divine thirsty mouth of hers the last dregs of a poor mortal life? They sought an insufficient refuge in Heraclitus' theory of opposites.

Meanwhile Troilus was always to be found at sunset, pacing up and down the walls by the western gate —quite mad. At dusk the Greek camp-fires would blossom along Xanthus banks—one after another, a myriad lights dancing in the dark.

As when the moon, refulgent lamp of night,
O'er heaven's pure azure spreads her something
   light.

He would repeat the simile to himself, but could never remember the correct epithets. Not that they mattered—any more than anything else.

IV

THERE are fine cities in the world—Manhattan, Ecbatana and Hecatompylus—but this city of Troy is the most fabulous of them all. Rome was seven hills of butcher's meat, Athens an abstraction of marble, in Alexandria the steam of kidney-puddings revolted the cœnobites, darkness and size render London inappreciable, Paris is full of sparrows, the snow lies gritty on Berlin, Moscow has no verisimilitude, all the East is peopled by masks and apes and larvæ. But this city of Troy is most of all real and fabulous with its charnel beauty.

"Is not Helen the end of our search—paradisal little World, symbol and epitome of the Great? Dawn sleeps in the transparent shadow of roses within her ear. The stainless candour of infinity—far-off peaks in summer and the Milky Way—has taken marvellous form in her. The Little World has its meteors, too, comets and shadowy clouds of hair, stars at whose glance men go planet-struck. Meteors —yes, and history it has. The past is still alive in the fragrance of her hair, and her young body breathes forth memories as old as the beginning of life—Eros first of gods. In her is the goal. I rest here with Helen."

"Fool," I said, "quote your Faustus. I go further."

V

FURTHER—but a hundred Liliputian tethers prevent me, the white nerves which tie soul to skin. And the whole air is aching with epidermical magnetism.

Further, further. But Troy is the birthplace of my homesickness. Troy is more than a patriotism, for it is built of my very flesh; the remembrance of it is a fire that sticks and tears when I would pull it off.

But further. One last look at Troilus where he stands by the western gate, staring over the plain. Further. When I have learnt the truth, I will return and build a new palace with domes less ominously like breasts, and there I will invent a safer Helen and a less paradoxical Cressid, and my harem will be a library for enlightenment.

VI

HERE are pagodas of diminishing bells. The leopard sleeps in the depth of his rosy cavern, and when he breathes it is a smell of irresistible sweetness; in the bestiaries he is the symbol of Christ in His sepulchre.

This listening conch has collected all the rumours of pantheism; the dew in this veined cup is the sacrament of nature, while these pale thuribles worship in the dark with yellow lamps and incense.

Everywhere alchemical profusion — the golden mintage of glades and ripples, vigils of passion enriched with silver under the fingers of the moon; everywhere lavishness, colour, music; the smoothness of machinery, incredible and fantastic ingenuities. God has lost his half-hunter in the desert.

But we have not come to worship among these Gothic beeches, for all their pillars and the lace-work of their green windows. We are looking for other things than churches.

VII

TREES, the half-fossilized exuberances of a passionate life, petrified fountains of intemperance—with their abolition begins the realm of reason.

Geometry, lines and planes, smooth edges, the ordered horror of perspectives. In this country there are pavements bright and sleek as water. The walls are precipices to which giants have nailed a perpetual cataract of marble. The fringes of the sky are scalloped with a pattern of domes and minarets. At night, too, the down-struck lamps are pyramids of phantom green and the perfect circle they make upon the pavement is magical.

Look over the parapet of the Acropolis. The bridges go dizzily down on their swaying catenaries, the gull's flight chained fast. The walls drop clear into the valley, all the millions of basalt blocks calcined into a single red monolith, fluted with thirstily shining organ pipes, which seem for ever wet. There are no crevices for moss and toad-flax, and even the claws of the yellow lichen slip on its polished flanks.

The valley is all paved and inlaid with rivers of steel. No trees, for they have been abolished.

"Glorious unnature," cries the watcher at the parapet. His voice launches into the abyss, following the curve of the bridges. "Glorious unnature. We have triumphed."

But his laughter as it descends is like a flight of broken steps.

VIII

LET us abandon ourselves to Time, which is beauty's essence. We live among the perpetual degenerations of apotheoses. Sunset dissolves into soft grey snow and the deep ocean of midnight, boundless as forgetfulness or some yet undiscovered Pacific, contracts into the green puddle of the dawn. The flowers burn to dust with their own brightness. On the banks of ancient rivers stand the pitiful stumps of huge towers and the ghosts of dead men straining to return into life. The woods are full of the smell of transience. Beauty, then, is that moment of descent when apotheosis tilts its wings downwards into the gulf. The ends of the curve lose themselves parabolically somewhere in infinity. Our sentimental eyes see only the middle section of this degeneration, knowing neither the upper nor the lower extremes, which some have thought to meet, godhead and annihilation.

Old Curiosity Shops! If I have said "Mortality is beauty," it was a weakness. The sense of time is a symptom of anæmia of the soul, through which flows angelic ichor. We must escape from the dust of the shop.

Cloistered darkness and sleep offer us their lotuses. Not to perceive where all is ugly, eaten into by the syphilis of time, heart-sickening—this is beauty; not to desire where death is the only consummation—wisdom.

Night is a measureless deep silence: daybreak brings back the fœtid gutters of the town. O supreme beauty of a night that knows no limitations—stars or the jagged edges of cock-crowing. Desperate, my mind has desired it: never my blood, whose pulse is a rhythm of the world.

At the other extreme, Beatrice lacks solidity, is as unresponsive to your kisses as mathematics. She too is an oubliette, not a way of life; an oubliette that, admittedly, shoots you upwards into light, not down to death; but it comes to the same thing in the end.

What, then, is the common measure? To take the world as it is, but metaphorically, informing the chaos of nature with a soul, qualifying transience with eternity.

When flowers are thoughts, and lonely poplars fountains of aspiring longing; when our actions are the poem of which all geographies and architectures and every science and all the unclassed individual odds and ends are the words, when even Helen's white voluptuousness matches some candour of the soul—then it will have been found, the permanent and living loveliness.

It is not a far-fetched, dear-bought gem; no pomander to be smelt only when the crowd becomes too stinkingly insistent; it is not a birth of rare oboes or violins, not visible only from ten to six by state permission at a nominal charge, not a thing richly apart, but an ethic, a way of belief and of practice, of faith and works, mediæval in its implication with the very threads of life. I desire no Paphian cloister of pink monks. Rather a rosy Brotherhood of Common Life, eating, drinking; marrying and giving in marriage;

taking and taken in adultery; reading, thinking, and when thinking fails, feeling immeasurably more subtly, sometimes perhaps creating.

Arduous search for one who is chained by his desires to dead carcases, whose eyes are dimmed with tears by the slow heart-breaking twilights full of old family ghosts laid in lavender, whose despair cries out for opiate and anodyne, craving gross sleep or a place on the airy unsupported pinnacles which hang in the sterile upper chambers of ether.

Ventre à terre, head in air—your centaurs are your only poets. Their hoofs strike sparks from the flints and they see both very near and immensely far.

SOLES OCCIDERE ET REDIRE POSSUNT

FOREWORD

JOHN RIDLEY, the subject of this poem, was killed in February 1918. "If I should perish," he wrote to me only five weeks before his death, "if I should perish—and one isn't exactly a 'good life' at the moment—I wish you'd write something about me. It isn't vanity (for I know you'll do me, if anything, rather less than justice!), not vanity, I repeat; but that queer irrational desire one has for immortality of any kind, however short and precarious—for frankly, my dear, I doubt whether your verses will be so very much more perennial than brass. Still, they'll be something. One can't, of course, believe in any *au-delà* for one's personal self; one would have first to believe in some kind of a friendly god. And as for being a spiritualist spook, one of those wretched beings who seem to spend their eternity in trying to communicate with the earth by a single telephone, where the number is always engaged, and the line chronically out of order—well, all I can say is, Heaven preserve me from such a future life. No, my only hope is you— and a damned poor guarantee for eternity. Don't make of me a khaki image, I beg. I'd rather you simply said of me, as Erasmus did of his brother, 'Strenuus compotor, nec scortator ignavus.' I sincerely hope, of course, that you won't have to write the thing at all—hope not, but have very little doubt you will. Good-bye."

The following poem is a tentative and provisional attempt to comply with his request. Ridley was an adolescent, and suffered from that instability of mind "produced by the mental conflict forced upon man by his sensitiveness to herd suggestion on the one hand and to experience on the other" (I quote from Mr. Trotter's memorable work on Herd Instinct), that characteristic instability which makes adolescence so feebly sceptical, so inefficient, so profoundly unhappy. I have fished up a single day from Ridley's forgotten existence. It has a bedraggled air in the sunlight, this poor wisp of Lethean weed. Fortunately, however, it will soon be allowed to drop back into the water, where we shall all, in due course, join it. "The greater part must be content to be as though they had not been."

I

BETWEEN the drawing of the blind
And being aware of yet another day
There came to him behind
Close, pregnant eyelids, like a flame of blue,
Intense, untroubled by the wind,
A Mediterranean bay,
Bearing a brazen beak and foamless oars
To where, marmoreally smooth and bright,
The steps soar up in one blue flight
From the sea's edge to the palace doors,
That have shut, have shut their valves of
        bronze—
And the windows too are lifeless eyes.

The galley grated on the stone;
He stepped out—and was alone:
No white-sailed hopes, no clouds, nor swans
To shatter the ocean's calm, to break the sky's.

Up the slow stairs:
                Did he know it was a dream?
First one foot up, then the other foot,
Shuddering like a mandrake root
That hears the truffle-dog at work
And draws a breath to scream;
To moan, to scream.
                The gates swing wide,
And it is coolly dark inside,
And corridors stretch out and out,

Joining the ceilings to their floors,
And parallels ring wedding bells
And through a hundred thousand doors
Perspective has abolished doubt.

But one of the doors was shut,
And behind it the subtlest lutanist
Was shaking a broken necklace of tinkling notes,
And somehow it was feminine music.
Strange exultant fear of desire, when hearts
Beat brokenly.   He laid his hand on the latch—
And woke among his familiar books and pictures;

Real as his dream?   He wondered.   Ten to nine.
Thursday.   Wasn't he lunching at his aunt's?
Distressing circumstance.
But then he was taking Jenny out to dine,
Which was some consolation.   What a chin!
Civilized ten thousand years, and still
No better way than rasping a pale mask
With imminent suicide, steel or obsidian:
Repulsive task!
And the more odious for being quotidian:
If one should live till eighty-five . . .
And the dead, do they still shave?   The horrible
      dead, are they alive?

But that lute, playing across his dream . . .
Quick drops breaking the sleep of the water-wheel,
Song and ebbing whisper of a summer stream,
Music's endless inconsequence that would reveal

To souls that listened for it, the all
Unseizable confidence, the mystic Rose,
Could it but find the magical fall
That droops, droops and dies into the perfect
     close . . .
And why so feminine?   But one could feel
The unseen woman sitting there behind
The door, making her ceaseless slow appeal
To all that prowls and growls in the caves beneath
The libraries and parlours of the mind.
If only one were rational, if only
At least one had the illusion of being so . . .

Nine o'clock.   Still in bed.   Warm, but how lonely!
He wept to think of all those single beds,
Those desperate night-long solitudes,
Those mental Salons full of nudes.
Shelley was great when he was twenty-four.
Eight thousand nights alone—minus, perhaps,
Six, or no! seven, certainly not more.
     Five little bits of heaven
       (Tum-de-rum, de-rum, de-rum),
Five little bits of heaven and one that was a
     lapse,
High-priced disgust: it stopped him suddenly
In the midst of laughter and talk with a tingling
     down the spine
(Like infants' impoliteness, a terrible infant's
     brightness),
And he would shut his eyes so as not to see
His own hot blushes calling him a swine.
Atrocious memory!   For memory should be

Of things secure and dead, being past,
Not living and disquieting.   At last
He threw the nightmare of his blankets off.

Cloudy ammonia, camels in your bath:
The earth hath bubbles as the water hath:
He was not of them, too, too solidly
Always himself.   What foam of kissing lips,
Pouting, parting with the ghost of the seven sips
One smacks for hiccoughs!
                                        Pitiable to be
Quite so deplorably naked when one strips.

There was his scar, a panel of old rose
Slashed in the elegant buff of his trunk hose;
Adonis punctured by his amorous boar,
Permanent souvenir of the Great War.
One of God's jokes, typically good,
That wound of his.   How perfect that he should
Have suffered it for—what?

II

OH, the dear front page of the *Times*!
Chronicle of essential history:
Marriage, birth, and the sly mysteriousness
Of lovers' greetings, of lovers' meetings,
And dirty death, impartially paid
To courage and the old decayed.
But nobody had been born to-day,
Nobody married that he knew,

Nobody died and nobody even killed;
  He felt a little aggrieved—
  Nobody even killed.
But, to make up: "Tuesday, Colchester train:
Wanted Brown Eyes' address, with a view to meeting
    again."
Dear Brown Eyes, it had been nice of her
To talk so friendly to a lonely traveller!
  Why is it nobody ever talks to me?

And now, here was a letter from Helen.
Better to open it rather than thus
Dwell in a long muse and maze
Over the scrawled address and the postmark,
Staring stupidly.
Love—was there no escape?
Was it always there, always there?
The same huge and dominant shape,
Like Windsor Castle leaning over the plain;
And the letter a vista cut through the musing forest,
At the end the old Round Tower,
Singing its refrain:
Here we are, here we are, here we are again!

The life so short, so vast love's science and art,
So many conditions of felicity.
  "Darling, will you become a part
  Of my poor physiology?
  And, my beloved, may I have
  The latchkey of your history?
  And while this corpse is what it is
  Dear, we must share geographies."

F

So many conditions of felicity.
And now time was a widening gulf and space,
A fixed between, and fate still kept them apart.
Her voice quite gone; distance had blurred her face.
The life so short, so vast love's science and art.

So many conditions—and yet, once,
Four whole days,
Four short days of perishing time,
They had fulfilled them all.
But that was long ago, ah! long ago,
Like the last horse bus, or the Christmas pantomime,
Or the Bells, oh, the Bells, of Edgar Allan Poe.

III

"HELEN, your letter, proving, I suppose,
That you exist somewhere in space, who knows?
Somewhere in time, perhaps, arrives this morning,
Reminding me with a note of Lutheran warning
That faith's the test, not works. Works!—any fool
Can do them if he tries to; but what school
Can teach one to credit the ridiculous,
The palpably non-existent? So with us,
Votaries of the copulative cult,
In this affair of love, *quicumque vult*,
Whoever would be saved, must love without
Adjunct of sense or reason, must not doubt
Although the deity be far removed,
Remote, invisible; who is not loved
Best by voluptuous works, but by the faith
That lives in absence and the body's death.

I have no faith, and even in love remain
Agnostic.   Are you here?   The fact is plain,
Constated by the heavenly vision of you,
Maybe by the mouth's warm touch; and that I love
    you,
I then most surely know, most painfully.
But now you've robbed the temple, leaving me
A poor invisibility to adore,
Now that, alas, you're vanished, gone . . . no
    more;
You take my drift.   I only ask your leave
To be a little unfaithful—not to you,
My dear, to whom I was and will be true,
But to your absence.   Hence no cause to grieve;
For absence may be cheated of a kiss—
Lightly and laughing—with no prejudice
To the so longed-for presence, which some day
Will crown the presence of

                    Le Vostre J.
(As dear unhappy Troilus would say)."

IV

OH, the maggots, the maggots in his brains!
Words, words and words.
A birth of rhymes and the strangest,
The most unlikely superfœtations—
New deep thoughts begot by a jingle upon a pun,
New worlds glimpsed through the window of a
    word
That has ceased, somehow, to be opaque.

All the muses buzzing in his head.
Autobiography crystallized under his pen, thus:

"When I was young enough not to know youth,
I was a Faun whose loves were Byzantine
Among stiff trees.   Before me naked Truth
Creaked on her intellectual legs, divine
In being inhuman, and was never caught
By all my speed; for she could outrun thought.

Now I am old enough to know I am young,
I chase more plastic beauties, but inspire
Life in their clay, purity in their dung
With the creative breath of my desire.
And utter truth is now made manifest
When on a certain sleeping face and breast

The moonlight dreams and silver chords are strung,
And a god's hand touches the aching lyre."

He read it through: a pretty, clinquant thing,
Like bright spontaneous bird-song in the spring,
Instinct with instinct, full of dewy freshness.
Yes, he had genius, if he chose to use it;
If he chose to—but it was too much trouble,
And he preferred reading.   He lit his pipe,
Opened his book, plunged in and soon was drowned
In pleasant seas . . . to rise again and find
One o'clock struck and his unshaven face
Still like a record in a musical box,
And Auntie Loo miles off in Bloomsbury.

V

I

THE Open Sesame of "Master John,"
And then the broad silk bosom of Aunt Loo.
"Dear John, this is a pleasure.   How are you?"
"Well, thanks.   Where's Uncle Will?"   "Your
      uncle's gone
To Bath for his lumbago.   He gets on
As well as anyone can hope to do
At his age—for you know he's seventy-two;
But still, he does his bit.   He sits upon

The local Tribunal at home, and takes
Parties of wounded soldiers out in brakes
To see the country.   And three times a week
He still goes up to business in the City;
And then, sometimes, at night he has to speak
In Village Halls for the War Aims Committee."

II

"Well, have you any news about the war?
What do they say in France?"   "I daren't repeat
The things they say."   "You see we've got some meat
For you, dear John.   Really, I think before
To-day I've had no lamb this year.   We score
By getting decent vegetables to eat,
Sent up from home.   This is a good receipt:
The touch of garlic makes it.   Have some more.

Poor Tom was wounded on the twenty-third;
Did you know that?   And just to-day I heard

News from your uncle that his nephew James
Is dead—Matilda's eldest boy." "I knew
One of those boys, but I'm so bad at names.
Mine had red hair." "Oh, now, that must be Hugh."

III

"Colonel McGillicuddy came to dine
Quietly here, a night or two ago.
He's on the Staff and very much in the know
About all sorts of things. His special line
Is Tanks. He says we've got a new design
Of super-Tank, with big guns, that can go
(I think he said) at thirty miles or so
An hour. That ought to make them whine

For peace. He also said, if I remember,
That the war couldn't last beyond September,
Because the Germans' trucks were wearing out
And couldn't be replaced. I only hope
It's true. You know your uncle has no doubt
That the whole thing was plotted by the Pope . . ."

". . . Good-bye, dear John. We *have* had a nice talk.
You must soon come again. Good-bye, good-
bye. . . ."

He tottered forth, full of the melancholy
That comes of surfeit, and began to walk
Slowly towards Oxford Street. The brazen sky
Burned overhead. Beneath his feet the stones
Were a grey incandescence, and his bones
Melted within hm, and his bowels yearned.

VI

THE crowd, the crowd—oh, he could almost cry
To see those myriad faces hurrying by,
And each a strong tower rooted in the past
On dark unknown foundations, each made fast
With locks nobody knew the secret of,
No key could open: save that perhaps love
Might push the bars half back and just peep in—
And see strange sights, it may be.   But for him
They were locked donjons, every window bright
With beckoning mystery; and then, Good Night!
The lamp was out, they were passed, they were gone
For ever . . . ever.   And one might have been
The hero or the friend long sought, and one
Was the loveliest face his eyes had ever seen,
(Vanished as soon) and he went lonely on.

Then in a sudden fearful vision he saw
The whole world spread before him—a vast sphere
Of seething atoms moving to one law:
"Be individual.   Approach, draw near,
Yes, even touch: but never join, never be
Other than your own selves eternally."
And there are tangents, tangents of thought that aim
Out through the gaps between the patterned stars
At some fantastic dream without a name
That like the moon shining through prison bars,
Visits the mind with madness.   So they fly,
Those soaring tangents, till the first jet tires,
Failing, faltering half-way up the sky,
And breaks—poor slender fountain that aspires

Against the whole strength of the heavy earth
Within whose womb, darkly, it took birth.

Oh, how remote he walked along the street,
Jostling with other lumps of human meat!

He was so tired. The café doors invite.
Caverned within them, still lingers the night
In shadowy coolness, soothing the seared sight.
He sat there smoking, soulless and wholly crass,
Sunk to the eyes in the warm sodden morass
Of his own guts, wearily, wearily
Ruminating visions of mortality—
Memento Moris from the pink alcove,
Nightmare oppressiveness of profane love.
Cesspool within, and without him he could see
Nothing but mounds of flesh and harlotry.
Like a half-pricked bubble pendulous in space,
The buttered leatheriness of a Jew's face
Looms through cigar-smoke; red and ghastly white,
Death's-head women fascinate the sight.
It was the nightmare of a corpse. Dead, dead . . .
Oh, to wake up, to live again! he fled
From that foul place and from himself.

VII

TWIN domes of the Alhambra,
Veiled tenderness of the sky above the Square:
He sat him down in the gardens, under the trees,
And in the dust, with the point of his umbrella,
Drew pictures of the crosses we have to bear.

The poor may starve, the sick have horrible
    pains—
But there are pale eyes even in the London
    planes.

Men may make war and money, mischief and love—
But about us are colours and the sky above.

Yes, here, where the golden domes ring clear,
And the planes patiently, hopefully renew
Their green refrain from year to year
To the dim spring burden of London's husky blue,
Here he could see the folly of it.   How?
Confine a boundless possible within
The prison of an ineluctable Now?
Go slave to pain, woo forth original sin
Out of her lair—and all by a foolish Act?
Madness! But now, Wordsworth of Leicester Square,
He'd learnt his lesson, learnt by the mere fact
Of the place existing, so finely unaware
Of syphilis and the restless in and out
Of public lavatories, and evening shout
Of winners and disasters, races and war.
Troubles come thick enough.   Why call for more
By suiting action to the divine Word?
His spleen was chronic, true; but he preferred
Its subtle agony to the brute force
That tugged the barbs of deep-anchored remorse.
The sunlight wrapped folds of soft golden silk
About him, and the air was warm as milk
Against his skin.   Long sitting still had made
Cramped soreness such a pleasure, he was afraid

To shift his tortured limbs, lest he should mar
Life's evenness.   London's noise from afar
Smoothed out its harshness to soothe his thoughts
    asleep,
Sound that made silence much more calm and
    deep.
The domes of gold, the leaves, emerald bright,
Were intense, piercing arrows of delight.
He did not think; thought was a shallow thing
To his deep sense of life, of mere being.
He looked at his hand, lying there on his knee,
The blue veins branching, the tendons cunningly
Dancing like jacks in a piano if he shook
A knot-boned finger.   Only to look and look,
Till he knew it, each hair and every pore—
It seemed enough: what need of anything more?
Thought, a blind alley; action, which at best
Is cudgelling water that goes back to rest
As soon as you give over your violences.
No, wisdom culls the flowers of the five senses,
Savouring the secret sweetness they afford:
Instead of which he had a Medical Board
Next week, and they would pass him fit. Good Lord!

Well, let all pass.
                    But one must outdo fate,
Wear clothes more modish than the fashion, run
Faster than time, not merely stand and wait;
Do in a flash what cannot be undone
Through ten eternities.   Predestinate?
So would God be—that is, if there were one:
General epidemic which spoils nobody's fun.

Action, action!   Quickly rise and do
The most irreparable things; beget,
In one brief consummation of the will,
Remorse, reaction, wretchedness, regret.
Action!   This was no time for sitting still.

He crushed his hat down over his eyes
And walked with a stamp to symbolize
Action, action—left, right, left;
Planting his feet with a slabby beat,
Taking strange Procrustean steps,
Lengthened, shortened to avoid
Touching the lines between the stones—
A thing which makes God so annoyed.

Action, action!   First of all
He spent three pounds he couldn't afford
In buying a book he didn't want,
For the mere sake of having been
Irrevocably extravagant.
Then feeling very bold, he pressed
The bell of a chance house; it might
Disclose some New Arabian Night
Behind its grimy husk, who knows?
The seconds passed; all was dead.
Arrogantly he rang once more.
His heart thumped on sheer silence; but at last
There was a shuffling; something behind the
     door
Became approaching panic, and he fled.

VIII

"MISERY," he said, "to have no chin,
Nothing but brains and sex and taste
Only omissively to sin,
Weakly kind and cowardly chaste.

But when the war is over,
I will go to the East and plant
Tea and rubber, and make much money.
I will eat the black sweat of niggers
And flagellate them with whips.
I shall be enormously myself,
    Incarnate Chin."

The anguish of thinking ill of oneself
(St. Paul's religion, poignant beyond words)
Turns ere you know it to faint minor thirds
Before the ritualistic pomps of the world—
The glass-grey silver of rivers, silken skies unfurled,
Urim and Thummim of dawn and sun-setting,
And the lawn sleeves of a great episcopal cloud,
Matins of song and vesperal murmuring,
Incense of night-long flowers and earth new-ploughed;
All beauties of sweetness and all that shine or sing.
Conscience is smoothed by beauty's subtle fingers
Into voluptuousness, where nothing lingers
Of bitterness, saving a sorrow that is
Rather a languor than a sense of pain.

So, from the tunnel of St. Martin's Lane
Sailing into the open Square, he felt
His self-reproach, his good resolutions melt

Into an ecstasy, gentle as balm,
Before the spire, etched black and white on the calm
Of a pale windless sky, St. Martin's spire,
And the shadows sleeping beneath the portico
And the crowd hurrying, ceaselessly, to and fro.
Alas, the bleached and slender tower that aches
Upon the gauzy sky, where blueness breaks
Into sweet hoarseness, veiled with love and tender
As the dove's voice alone in the woods: too slender,
Too finely pencilled—black and bleaching white
On smoky mist, too clear in the keen light
Of utmost summer: and oh! the lives that pass
In one swift stream of colour, too, too bright,
Too swift—and all the lives unknown,

Alone.

Alas. . . .

A truce to summer and beauty and the pain
Of being too consciously alive among
The things that pass and the things that remain,
(Oh, equal sadness!) the pain of being young.

Truce, truce. . . . Once again he fled;—
All his life, it seemed, was a flight;—
Fled and found
Sanctuary in a cinema house.
Huge faces loomed and burst,
Like bubbles in a black wind.
He shut his eyes on them and in a little
Slept; slept, while the pictures
Passed and returned, passed once more and returned.
And he, like God in the midst of the wheeling world,

Slept on; and when he woke it was eight o'clock.
Jenny? Revenge is sweet; he will have kept
  Dear Jenny waiting.

IX

TALL straight poplars stand in a meadow;
The wind and sun caress them, dappling
The deep green grass with shine and shadow;
And a little apart one slender sapling
Sways in the wind and almost seems
Conscious of its own supple grace,
And shakes its twin-hued leaves and gleams
With silvery laughter, filling the place
Where it stands with a sudden flash of human
Beauty and grace; till from her tree
Steps forth the dryad, now turned woman,
And sways to meet him.   It is she.

Food and drink, food and drink:
Olives as firm and sleek and green
As the breasts of a sea-god's daughter,
Swimming far down where the corpses sink
Through the dense shadowy water.
Silver and black on flank and back,
The glossy sardine mourns its head.
The red anchovy and the beetroot red,
With carrots, build a gorgeous stair—
Bronze, apoplexy and Venetian hair—
And the green pallor of the salad round
Sharpens their clarion sound.

De lady take hors d'œuvres? and de gentleman too?
Per due! Due! Echo answers: Du' . . .

"So, Jenny, you've found another Perfect Man."
"Perfect, perhaps; but not so sweet as you,
Not such a baby." "Me? A baby. Why,
I am older than the rocks on which I sit. . . ."
    Oh, how delightful, talking about oneself!

Golden wine, pale as a Tuscan primitive,
And wine's strange taste, half loathsome, half
     delicious:
Come, my Lesbia, let us love and live.
What though the mind still think that one thing's
     vicious
More than another? If the thought can give
This wine's rich savour to our laughing kiss,
Let us preserve the Christian prejudice.
Oh, there are shynesses and silences,
Shynesses and silences!
But luckily God also gave us wine.

"Jenny, adorable—" (what draws the line
At the mere word "love"?) "has anyone the right
To look so lovely as you look to-night,
To have such eyes, such a helmet of bright hair?"
But candidly, he wondered, do I care?

He heard her voice and himself spoke,
But like faint light through a cloud of smoke,
There came, unreal and far away,
Mere sounds utterly empty—like the drone

Of prayers, *crambe repetita*, prayers and praise,
Long, long ago, in the old School Chapel days;
Senseless, but so intrusive on one's own
Interior life one couldn't even think . . .

O sweet, rare, perilous, retchy drink!
Another glass . . .

X

How cool is the moonless summer night, how sweet
After the noise and the dizzy choking heat!
The bloodless lamps look down upon their own
Green image in the polished roadway thrown,
And onward and out of sight the great road runs,
Smooth and dark as a river of calm bronze.

Freedom and widening space: his life expands,
Ready, it seems, to burst the iron bands
Of self, to fuse with other lives and be
Not one but the world, no longer "I" but "She."

See, like the dolorous memory
Of happy times in misery,
An aged hansom fills the street
With the superannuated beat
Of hollow hoofs and bells that chime
Out of another quieter time.

"Good-night," the last kiss, "and God bless you, my
        dear."
So, she was gone, she who had been so near,

So breathing-warm—soft mouth and hands and hair—
A moment since.   Had she been really there,
Close at his side, and had he kissed her?   It seemed
Unlikely as something somebody else had dreamed
And talked about at breakfast, being a bore:
Improbable, unsubstantial, dim, yet more
Real than the rest of life; real as the blaze
Of a sudden-seen picture, as the lightning phrase
With which the poet-gods strangely create
Their brief bright world beyond the reach of fate.
Yet he could wonder now if he had kissed
Her or his own loved thoughts.   Did she exist
Now she was history and safely stowed
Down in the past?   There (with a conscious smile),
There let her rest eternal.   And meanwhile,
Lamp-fringed towards meeting parallels, the road
Stretched out and out, and the old weary horse,
Come from the past, went jogging his homeward
      course
Uphill through time to some demoded place,
On ghostly hoofs back to the safe Has-Been:—
But fact returns insistent as remorse;
Uphill towards Hampstead, back to the year of grace
Nineteen hundred and seventeen.

XI

BETWEEN the drawing of the blind
And being aware of yet another day . . .

THE CICADAS

THEATRE OF VARIETIES

CIRCLE on circle the hanging gardens descend,
Sloping from upper darkness, each flower face
Open, turned to the light and laughter and life
Of the sun-like stage.   And all the space between,
Like the hot fringes of a summer sky,
Is quick with trumpets, beats with the pulse of
     drums,
Athwart whose sultry thunders rise and fall
Flute fountains and the swallow flight of strings.
Music, the revelation and marvellous lie!
On the bright trestles tumblers, tamers of beasts,
Dancers and clowns affirm their fury of life.

     "The World-Renowned Van Hogen Mogen in
         The Master Mystery of Modern Times."

He talks, he talks; more powerfully than even
Music his quick words hammer on men's minds.
"Observe this hat, ladies and gentlemen;
Empty, observe, empty as the universe
Before the Head for which this Hat is made
Was or could think.   Empty, observe, observe."
The rabbit kicks; a bunch of paper flowers
Blooms in the limelight; paper tape unrolls,
Endless, a clue.   "Ladies and gentlemen . . ."
Sharp, sharp on malleable minds his words
Hammer.   The little Indian boy
Enters the basket.   Bright, an Ethiop's sword
Transfixes it and bleeding is withdrawn.

Death draws and petrifies the watching faces.
"Ladies and gentlemen": the great Van Hogen
  Mogen
Smiles and is kind. A puddle of dark blood
Slowly expands. "The irremediable
Has been and is no more."
Empty of all but blood, the basket gapes.
"Arise!" he calls, and blows his horn. "Arise!"
And bird-like from the highest gallery
The little Indian answers.
Shout upon shout, the hanging gardens rever-
  berate.
Happy because the irremediable is healed,
Happy because they have seen the impossible,
Because they are freed from the dull daily law,
They shout, they shout. And great Van Hogen
  Mogen
Modestly bows, graciously smiles. The band
Confirms the lie with cymbals and bassoons,
The curtain falls. How quickly the walls recede,
How soon the petrified gargoyles re-become
Women and men! who fill the warm thick air
With rumour of their loves and discontents,
Not suffering even great Hogen Mogen—
Only begetter out of empty hats
Of rose and rabbit, raiser from the dead—
To invade the sanctity of private life.

The Six Aerial Sisters Polpetini
Dive dangerously from trapeze to far
Trapeze, like stars, and know not how to fall.
For if they did and if, of his silver balls,

Sclopis, the juggler, dropped but one—but one
Of all the flying atoms which he builds
With his quick throwing into a solid arch—
What panic then would shake the pale flower
      faces
Blooming so tranquilly in their hanging beds!
What a cold blast of fear!   But patrons must not,
And since they must not, cannot be alarmed.
Hence Sclopis, hence (the proof is manifest)
The Six Aerial Ones infallibly
Function, and have done, and for ever will.

Professor Chubb's Automaton performs
Upon the viols and virginals, plays chess,
Ombre and loo, mistigri, tric-trac, pushpin,
Sings Lilliburlero in falsetto, answers
All questions put to it, and with its rubber feet
Noiselessly dances the antique heydiguy.
"Is it a man?" the terrible infant wonders.
And "no," they say, whose business it is
To say such infants nay.   And "no" again
They shout when, after watching Dobbs and Debs
Step simultaneously through intricate dances,
Hammer the same tune with their rattling clogs
In faultless unison, the infant asks,
"And they, are they machines?"

Music, the revelation and marvellous lie,
Rebuilds in the minds of all a suave and curving
Kingdom of Heaven, where the saxophone
Affirms everlasting loves, the drums deny

Death, and where great Tenorio, when he sings,
Makes Picardy bloom only with perfumed roses,
And never a rotting corpse in all its earth.
Play, music, play! In God's bright limelight eyes
An angel walks and with one rolling glance
Blesses each hungry flower in the hanging
    gardens.
"Divine," they cry, having no words by which
To call the nameless spade a spade, "Divine
Zenocrate!" There are dark mysteries
Whose name is beauty, strange revelations called
Love, and a gulph of pleasure and of awe
Where words fall vain and wingless in the dark;
The seen Ineffable, the felt but all-Unknown
And Undescribed, is God.   "Divine, divine!"
The god-intoxicated shout goes up.
"Divine Zenocrate!"
"Father," the terrible infant's voice is shrill,
"Say, father, why does the lady wear no skirts?"
She wears no skirts; God's eyes have never been
    brighter.
The face flowers open in her emanation.
She is the suave and curving Kingdom of Heaven
Made visible, and in her sugared song
The ear finds paradise.   Divine, divine!
Her belly is like a mound of wheat, her breasts
Are towers, her hair like a flock of goats.
  Her foot is feat with diamond toes
   And she—divine Zenocrate—
   And she on legs of ruby goes.
The face flowers tremble in the rushing wind
Of her loud singing.   A poet in the pit

Jots down in tears the words of her Siren song.
  So every spirit as it is most pure,
    And hath in it the more of heavenly light,
  So it the rarer body doth procure
    To habit in, and is more fairly dight
    With cheerful grace and amiable sight:
    For of the soul the body form doth take;
    And soul is form and doth the body make.
"Now, boys, together.   All with me," she cries
Through the long sweet suspense of dominant
      chords;
"For of the soul," her voice is paradise,
"For of the soul the body form doth take;
And soul is form and doth the body make."
Zenocrate, alone, alone divine!

God save the King.   Music's last practical joke
Still bugling in their ears of war and glory,
The folk emerge into the night.
Already next week's bills are being posted:—
Urim and Thummim, cross-talk comedians;
Ringpok, the Magian of Tibet;
The Two Bedelias; Ruby and Truby Dix;
Sam Foy and Troupe of Serio-Comic Cyclists . . .
Theatre of immemorial varieties,
Old mummery, but mummers never the same!
Twice nightly every night from now till doomsday
The hanging gardens, bedded with pale flower
      faces,
Young flowers in the old old gardens, will echo
With ever new, with ever new delight.

PICTURE BY GOYA

A HIGHWAY ROBBERY

IT is a scene of murder—elegant, is it not?
You lutanists, who play to naked Queens,
As summer sleep or music under trees,
As luncheon on the grass—the grass on which
The country copulatives make sport, the pale
Grass with the tall tubed hats, the inky coats
And rosy, rosy among the funeral black
(*Memento Vivere*) a naked girl.
But here the sleepers bleed, the tumbling couples
Struggle, but not in love; the naked girl
Kneels at the feet of one who hesitates,
Voluptuously, between a rape and a murder.

Bandits angelical and you, rich corpses!
Truth is your sister, Goodness your spouse.
Towering skies lean down and tall, tall trees
Impose their pale arsenical benediction,
Making all seem exquisitely remote
And small and silent, like a village fair
Seen from the hill-top, far far below.
And yet they walk on the village green to whom
The fair is huge, tumultuous, formidable.   Earth
Lies unremembered beneath the feet of dancers
Who, looking up, see not the sky, but towers
And bright invading domes and the fierce swings,
Scythe-like, reaping and ravaging the quiet.
And when night falls, the shuddering gas-flares scoop

Out of the topless dark a little vault
Of smoky gold, wherein the dancers still
Jig away, gods of a home-made universe.

CALIGULA

OR THE TRIUMPH OF BEAUTY

PROW after prow, the floating ships
Bridge the blue gulph; the road is laid;
And Cæsar on a piebald horse
Prances with all his cavalcade.

Drunk with their own quick blood they go.
The waves flash as with seeing eyes;
The tumbling cliffs mimic their speed,
And they have filled the vacant skies

With waltzing Gods and Virtues, set
Æolus roaring with their shout,
Made Vesta's temple on the cape
Spin like a circus roundabout.

The twined caduceus in his hand,
And having golden wings for spurs,
Young Cæsar dressed as God looks on
And cheers his jolly mariners;

Cheers as they heave from off the bridge
The trippers from the seaside town;
Laughs as they bang the bobbing heads
And shove them bubbling down to drown.

There sweeps a spiral curve of gesture
From the allegoric sky;
Beauty, like conscious lightning, runs
Through Jove's ribbed trunk and Juno's thigh,

Slides down the flank of Mars and takes
From Virtue's rump a dizzier twist,
Licks round a cloud and whirling stoops
Earthwards to Cæsar's lifted fist.

A burgess tumbles from the bridge
Headlong, and hurrying Beauty slips
From Cæsar through the plunging legs
To the blue sea between the ships.

NERO AND SPORUS

OR THE TRIUMPH OF ART

THE Christians by whose muddy light
Dimly, dimly I divine
Your eyes and see your pallid beauty
Like a pale night-primrose shine,

Colourless in the dark, revere
A God who slowly died that they
Might suffer the less, who bore the pain
Of all time in a single day,
The pain of all men in a single
Wounded body and sad heart.

The yellow marble, smooth as water,
Builds me a Golden House; and there
The marble Gods sleep in their strength
And the white Parian girls are fair.

Roses and waxen oleanders,
Green grape bunches and the flushed peach—
All beautiful things I taste, touch, see,
Knowing, loving, becoming each.

The ship went down, my mother swam:
I wedded and myself was wed:
Old Claudius died of emperor-bane:
Old Seneca too slowly bled.

The wild beast and the victim both,
The ravisher and the wincing bride,
King of the world and a slave's slave,
Terror-haunted, deified——

All these, sweet Sporus, I, an artist,
Am and, an artist, needs must be.
Is the tune Lydian?   I have loved you.
And you have heard my symphony

Of wailing voices and clashed brass,
With long shrill flutings that suspend
Pain o'er a muttering gulph of terrors,
And piercing blasts of joy that end,

Gods, in what discord!—could I have
So hymned the Furies, were the bane
Still sap within the hemlock stalk,
The red swords virgin-bright again?

Or take a child's love that is all
Worship, all tenderness and trust,
A dawn-web, dewy and fragile—take
And with the violence of lust

Tear and defile it.   You shall hear
The breaking dumbness and the thin
Harsh crying that is the very music
Of shame and the remorse of sin.

Christ died; the artist lives for all;
Loves, and his naked marbles stand
Pure as a column on the sky,
Whose lips, whose breasts, whose thighs demand

Not our humiliation, not
The shuddering of an after-shame;
And of his agonies men know
Only the beauty born of them.

Christ died, but living Nero turns
Your mute remorse to song; he gives
To idiot Fate eyes like a lover's,
And while his music plays, God lives.

NERO AND SPORUS

II

DARK stirrings in the perfumed air
Touch your cheeks, lift your hair.
With softer fingers I caress,
Sporus, all your loveliness.
Round as a fruit, tree-tangled shines
The moon; and fire-flies in the vines,
Like stars in a delirious sky,
Gleam and go out.   Unceasingly
The fountains fall, the nightingales
Sing.   But time flows and love avails
Nothing.   The Christians smoulder red;
Their brave blue-hearted flames are dead;
And you, sweet Sporus, you and I
We too must die, we too must die.

MYTHOLOGICAL INCIDENT

THROUGH the pale skeleton of woods
Orion walks.   The North Wind lays
Its cold lips to the twin steel flutes
That are his gun, and plays.

Knee-deep he goes, where penny-wiser
Than all his kind who steal and hoard,
Year after year some sylvan miser
His copper wealth has stored.

The Queen of Love and Beauty lays
In neighbouring beechen aisles her baits—
Bread-crumbs and the golden maize.
Patiently she waits.

And when the unwary pheasant comes
To fill his painted maw with crumbs,
Accurately the sporting Queen
Takes aim.   The bird has been.

Secure, Orion walks her way.
The Cyprian loads, presents, makes fire.
He falls.   'Tis Venus all entire
Attached to her recumbent prey.

FEMMES DAMNÉES

(From the French of Charles Baudelaire)

THE lamps had languisht and their light was pale;
On cushions deep Hippolyta reclined.
Those potent kisses that had torn the veil
From her young candour filled her dreaming mind.

With tempest-troubled eyes she sought the blue
Heaven of her innocence, how far away!
Like some sad traveller, who turns to view
The dim horizons passed at dawn of day.

Tears and the muffled light of weary eyes,
The stupor and the dull voluptuous trance,
Limp arms, like weapons dropped by one who flies—
All served her fragile beauty to enhance.

Calm at her feet and joyful, Delphine lay
And gazed at her with ardent eyes and bright,
Like some strong beast that, having mauled its prey,
Draws back to mark the imprint of its bite.

Strong and yet bowed, superbly on her knees,
She snuffed her triumph, on that frailer grace
Poring voluptuously, as though to seize
The signs of thanks upon the other's face.

Gazing, she sought in her pale victim's eye
The speechless canticle that pleasure sings,
The infinite gratitude that, like a sigh,
Mounts slowly from the spirit's deepest springs.

"Now, now you understand (for love like ours
Is proof enough) that 'twere a sin to throw
The sacred holocaust of your first flowers
To those whose breath might parch them as they blow.

"Light falls my kiss, as the ephemeral wing
That scarcely stirs the shining of a lake.
What ruinous pain your lover's kiss would bring!
A plough that leaves a furrow in its wake.

"Over you, like a herd of ponderous kine,
Man's love will pass and his caresses fall
Like trampling hooves. Then turn your face to mine;
Turn, oh my heart, my half of me, my all!

"Turn, turn, that I may see their starry lights,
Your eyes of azure; turn. For one dear glance
I will reveal love's most obscure delights,
And you shall drowse in pleasure's endless trance."

"Not thankless, nor repentant in the least
Is your Hippolyta." She raised her head.
"But one who from some grim nocturnal feast
Returns at dawn feels less disquieted.

"I bear a weight of terrors, and dark hosts
Of phantoms haunt my steps and seem to lead.
I walk, compelled, behind these beckoning ghosts
Down sliding roads and under skies that bleed.

"Is ours so strange an act, so full of shame?
Explain the terrors that disturb my bliss.
When you say, Love, I tremble at the name;
And yet my mouth is thirsty for your kiss.

"Ah, look not so, dear sister, look not so!
You whom I love, even though that love should be
A snare for my undoing, even though
Loving I am lost for all eternity."

H

Delphine looked up, and fate was in her eye.
From the god's tripod and beneath his spell,
Shaking her tragic locks, she made reply:
"Who in love's presence dares to speak of hell?

"Thinker of useless thoughts, let him be cursed,
Who in his folly, venturing to vex
A question answerless and barren, first
With wrong and right involved the things of sex!

"He who in mystical accord conjoins
Shadow with heat, dusk with the noon's high fire,
Shall never warm the palsy of his loins
At that red sun which mortals call desire.

"Go, seek some lubber groom's deflowering lust;
Take him your heart and leave me here despised!
Go—and bring back, all horror and disgust,
The livid breasts man's love has stigmatized.

"One may not serve two masters here below."
But the child answered: "I am torn apart,
I feel my inmost being rent, as though
A gulf had yawned—the gulf that is my heart.

"Naught may this monster's desperate thirst
      assuage,—
As fire 'tis hot, as space itself profound—
Naught save the Fury from her quenchless rage,
Who with her torch explores its bleeding wound.

"Curtain the world away and let us try
If lassitude will bring the boon of rest.
In your deep bosom I would sink and die,
Would find the grave's fresh coolness on your breast."

Hence, lamentable victims, get you hence!
Hell yawns beneath, your road is straight and steep.
Where all the crimes receive their recompense
Wind-whipped and seething in the lowest deep

With a huge roaring as of storms and fires,
Go down, mad phantoms, doomed to seek in vain
The ne'er-won goal of unassuaged desires,
And in your pleasures find eternal pain!

Sunless your caverns are; the fever damps
That filter in through every crannied vent
Break out with marsh-fire into sudden lamps
And steep your bodies with their frightful scent.

The barrenness of pleasures harsh and stale
Makes mad your thirst and parches up your skin;
And like an old flag volleying in the gale,
Your whole flesh shudders in the blasts of sin.

Far from your kind, outlawed and reprobate,
Go, prowl like wolves through desert worlds apart!
Disordered souls, fashion your own dark fate,
And flee the god you carry in your heart.

ARABIA INFELIX

UNDER a ceiling of cobalt
And mirrored by as void a blue,
Wet only with the wind-blown salt,
The Arabian land implores a dew.

Parched, parched are the hills, and dumb
That thundering voice of the ravine;
Round the dead springs the birds are seen
No more, no more at evening come

(Like lovely thoughts to one who dwells
In quiet, like enchanting hopes)
The leopards and the shy gazelles
And the light-footed antelopes.

Death starts at every rattling gust
That in the withered torrent's bed
Whirls up a phantom of grey dust
And, dying, lets the ghost fall dead.

Dust in a dance may seem to live;
But laid, not blown, it brings to birth.
Not wind, but only rain can give
Life, and to a patient earth.

Hot wind from this Arabian land
Chases the clouds, withholds the rain.
No footstep prints the restless sand
Wherein who sows, he sows in vain.

If there were water, if there were
But a shower, a little fountain springing,
How rich would be the perfumed air,
And the green woods with shade and singing.

Bright hills, but by the sun accursed,
Peaceful, but with the peace of hell—
Once on these barren slopes there fell
A plague more violent than thirst:

Anguish to kill inveterate pain
And mortal slaking of desire;
Dew, and a long-awaited rain—
A dew of blood, a rain of fire.

Into a vacant sky the moist
Grey pledge of spring and coming leaves
Swam, and the thirsty hills rejoiced,
All golden with their future sheaves.

Flower-phantoms in the parching air
Nodded, and trees ungrown were bowed;
With love like madness, like despair,
The mountain yearned towards the cloud.

And she in silence slowly came,
Oh! to transfigure, to renew,
Came laden with a gift of dew,
But with it dropped the lightning's flame;

A flame that rent the crags apart,
But rending made a road between
For water to the mountain's heart,
That left a scar, but left it green.

Faithless the cloud and fugitive;
An empty heaven nor burns, nor wets;
At peace, the barren land regrets
Those agonies that made it live.

THE MOOR

CHAMPION of souls and holiness, upholder
Of all the virtues, father of the Church,
Honest, honest, honest Iago! how
Crusadingly, with what indignant zeal
(*Ora pro nobis*), caracoling on
Your high horse and emblazoned, gules on white,
Did you ride forth (Oh, pray for us), ride forth
Against the dark-skinned hosts of evil, ride,
Martyr and saint, against those paynim hosts,
Having for shield all Sinai, and for sword,
To smite rebellion and avenge the Lord,
The sharp, the shining certainty of faith!
(*Ora pro nobis*) point us out the Way.

" Lily bright and stinking mud:
Fair is fair and foul is ill.
With her, on her, what you will.
This fire must be put out with blood,
Put out with blood."

But for a glint, a hint of questing eyes,
Invisible, darkness through darkness goes
On feet that even in their victim's dreaming
Wake not an echo.
Lost, he is lost; and yet thus wholly in darkness
Melted, the Moor is more Othello than when,
Green-glittering, the sharp Venetian day
Revealed him armed and kingly and commanding
Captain of men.

How still she lies, this naked Desdemona,
All but a child and sleeping and alone,
How still and white!
Whose breast, whose arms, the very trustfulness
Of her closed eyelids and unhurried breath
More than a philtre maddeningly invite
Lust and those hands, those huge dark hands, and
death.

"For oh, the lily and the mud!
Fair is still fair and foulness, ill.
With her, on her, what you will.
This fire must be put out with blood."

Well, now the fire is out, and the light too;
All, all put out. In Desdemona's place
Lies now a carrion. That fixed grimace
Of lidless eyes and starting tongue
Derides his foolishness. Cover her face;
This thing but now was beautiful and young.

Honest Iago's Christian work is over;
Short, short the parleying at the Golden Gate.
"For I am one who made the Night ashamed
Of his own essence, that his dark was dark;
One who with good St. Jerome's filthy tongue
Tainted desire and taught the Moor to scorn
His love's pale body, and because she had
Lain gladly in his arms, to call her whore
And strangle her for whoredom." So he spoke,
And with majestic motion heaven's high door
Rolled musically apart its burnished vans
To grant him entrance.

                      Turning back meanwhile
From outer darkness, Othello and his bride
Perceive the globe of heaven like one small lamp
Burning alone at midnight in the abyss
Of some cathedral cavern; pause, and then
With face once more averted, hand in hand,
Explore the unseen treasures of the dark.

NOBLEST ROMANS

COLUMNS and unageing fountains,
Jets of frost and living foam—
Let them leap from seven mountains,
The seven hills of Rome.

Flanked by arch and echoing arch,
Let the streets in triumph go;
Bid the aqueducts to march
Tireless through the plain below.

Column-high in the blue air,
Let the marble Cæsars stand;
Let the gods, who living were
Romans, lift a golden hand.

Many, but each alone, a crowd,
Yet of Romans, throng their shrine;
Worshippers themselves divine,
Gods to gods superbly bowed;

Romans bowed to shapes that they,
Sculptors of the mind, set free;
Supplicant that they may be
Peers of those to whom they pray.

ORION

TREE-TANGLED still, autumn Orion climbs
Up from among the North Wind's shuddering emblems
Into the torrent void
And dark abstraction of invisible power,
The heart and boreal substance of the night.

Pleione flees before him, and behind,
Still sunken, but prophetically near,
Death in the Scorpion hunts him up the sky
And round the vault of time, round the slow-curving
    year,
Follows unescapably
And to the end, aye, and beyond the end
Will follow, follow; for of all the gods
Death only cannot die.

The rest are mortal.   And how many lie
Already with their creatures' ancient dust!
Dead even in us who live—or hardly live,
Since of our hearts impiety has made,
Not tombs indeed (for they are holy; tombs
Secretly live with everlasting Death's
Dark and mysterious life),
But curious shops and learned lumber rooms
Of bone and stone and every mummied thing,
Where Death himself his sacred sting
Forgets (how studiously forgotten
Amid the irrelevant to and fro of feet!),
Where by the peeping and the chattering,
The loud forgetfulness seemingly slain,
He lies with all the rest—and yet we know,
In secret yet we know,
Death is not dead, not dead but only sleeping,
And soon will rise again.

Not so the rest.   Only the Scorpion burns
In our unpeopled heaven of empty names
And insubstantial echoes; only Death
Still claims our prayers, and still to those who pray
Returns his own dark blood and quickening breath,
Returns the ominous mystery of fear.
Where are the gods of dancing and desire?
Anger and joy, laughter and tears and wine,
Those other mysteries of fire and flame,
Those more divine than Death's—ah, where are
     they?
Only a ghost between the shuddering trees,
Only a name and ghostly numbers climb;

And where a god pursued and fled,
Only a ghostly time, a ghostly place
Attends on other ghostly times and places.
Orion and the rest are dead.

And yet to-night, here in the exulting wind,
Amid the enormous laughters of a soul
At once the world's and mine,
God-like Orion and all his brother stars
Shine as with living eyes,
With eyes that glance a recognition, glance a sign
Across the quickened dark, across the gulphs
That separate no more,
But, like wide seas that yet bring home the freight
Of man's mad yearning for a further shore,
Join with a living touch, unbrokenly,
Life to mysterious life,
The Hunter's alien essence to my own.

Orion lives; yet I who know him living,
Elsewhere and otherwise
Know him for dead, and dead beyond all hope,
For 'tis the infertile and unquickening death
Of measured places and recorded times,
The death of names and numbers that he dies.
Only the phantom of Orion climbs.
Put out the eyes, put out the living eyes
And look elsewhere; yes, look and think and be
Elsewhere and otherwise.
But *here* and *thus* are also in their right,
Are in their right divine to send this wind of laughter
Rushing through the cloudless dark

And through my being; have a right divine
And imprescriptible now to reveal
The starry god, a right to make me feel,
As even now, as even now I feel,
His living presence near me in the night.

A curved and figured glass hangs between light and
    light,
Between the glow within us and the glow
Of what mysterious sun without?
Vast over earth and sky, or focussed burningly
Upon the tender quick, our spirits throw
Each way their images—each way the forms
O! shall it be of beauty, shall it be
The naked skeletons of doubt?
Or else, symbolically dark, the cloudy forms
Of mystery, or dark (but dark with death)
Shapes of sad knowledge and defiling hate? .

"Lighten our darkness, Lord." With what pure
    faith,
What confident hope our fathers once implored
The Light! But 'tis the shitten Lord of Flies
Who with his loathsome bounties now fulfils
On us their prayers. Our fathers prayed for light.
Through windows at their supplication scoured
Bare of the sacred blazons, but instead
Daubed with the dung-god's filth, all living eyes,
Whether of stars or men, look merely dead;
While on the vaulted crystal of the night
Our guttering souls project,

Not the Wild Huntsman, not the Heavenly Hosts,
But only times and places, only names and ghosts.

And yet, for all the learned Lord of Dung,
The choice is ours, the choice is always ours,
To see or not to see the living powers
That move behind the numbered points and times.
The Fly King rules; but still the choice remains
With us his subjects, we are free, are free
To love our fate or loathe it; to rejoice
Or weep or wearily accept; are free,
For all the scouring of our souls, for all
The miring of their crystal, free to give
Even to an empty sky, to vacant names,
Or not to give, our worship; free to turn
Lifewards, within, without, to what transcends
The squalor of our personal ends and aims,
Or not to turn; yes, free to die or live;
Free to be thus and passionately here,
Or otherwise and otherwhere;
Free, in a word, to learn or not to learn
The art to think and musically do
And feel and be, the never more than now
Difficult art harmoniously to live
All poetry—the midnight of Macbeth
And ripe Odysseus and the undying light
Of Gemma's star and Cleopatra's death
And Falstaff in his cups; the art to live
That discipline of flowers, that solemn dance
Of sliding weights and harnessed powers
Which is a picture; or to live the grave
And stoical recession, row on row,

Of equal columns, live the passionate leaping,
The mutual yearning, meeting, marrying,
And then the flame-still rapture, the fierce trance
Of consummation in the Gothic night.

The choice is always ours.   Then, let me choose
The longest art, the hard Promethean way
Cherishingly to tend and feed and fan
That inward fire, whose small precarious flame,
Kindled or quenched, creates
The noble or the ignoble men we are,
The worlds we live in and the very fates,
Our bright or muddy star.

Up from among the emblems of the wind
Into its heart of power,
The Huntsman climbs, and all his living stars
Are bright, and all are mine.

MEDITATION

WHAT now caresses you, a year ago
Bent to the wind that sends a travelling wave
Almost of silver through the silky corn
Westward of Calgary; or two weeks since
Bleated in Gloster market, lowed at Thame,
And slowly bled to give my lips desire;
Or in the teeming darkness, fathoms down,
Hung, one of millions, poised between the ooze
And the wind's foamy skirts; or feathered flew,
Or deathwards ran before the following gun.

And all day long, knee deep in the wet grass,
The piebald cows of Edam chewed and chewed,
That what was cheese might pulse thus feverishly;
And now, prophetically, even now
They ponder in their ruminating jaws
My future body, which in Tuscan fields
Yet grows, yet grunts among the acorns, yet
Is salt and iron, water and touchless air,
Is only numbers variously moved,
Is nothing, yet will love your nothingness.
Vast forms of dust, tawny and tall and vague,
March through the desert, creatures of the wind.
Wind, blowing whither, blowing whence, who
    knows?—
Wind was the soul that raised them from the sand,
Moved and sustained their movement, and at last
Abating, let them fall in separate grains
Slowly to earth and left an empty sky.

SEPTEMBER

SPRING is past and over these many days,
Spring and summer. The leaves of September
    droop,
Yellowing and all but dead in the patient trees.
Nor is there any hope in me. I walk
Slowly homewards. Night is as empty and dark
Behind my eyes as it is dark without
And empty round about me and over me.
Spring is past and over these many days,
But, looking up, suddenly I see

Leaves in the upthrown light of a street lamp
    shining,
Clear and luminous, young and so transparent,
They seem but the coloured foam of air, green fire,
No more than the scarce-embodied thoughts of
    leaves.
And it is spring within that circle of light.
Oh, magical brightness! The old leaves are made
    new.
In the mind, too, some coloured accident
Of beauty revives and makes all young again,
A chance light shines and suddenly it is spring.

SEASONS

BLOOD of the world, time stanchless flows;
The wound is mortal and is mine.
I act, but not to my design,
Choose, but 'twas ever fate that chose,
Would flee, but there are doors that close.
Winter has set its muddy sign
Without me and within. The rose
Dies also in my heart and no stars shine.

But nightingales call back the sun;
The doors are down and I can run,
Can laugh, for destiny is dead.
All springs are hoarded in the flowers;
Quick flow the intoxicating hours,
For wine as well as blood is red.

STORM AT NIGHT

OH, how aquarium-still, how brooding-warm
This paradise!   How peacefully in the womb
Of war itself, and at the heart of storm
How safely—safely a captive, in a tomb—
I lie and, listening to the wild assault,
The pause and once-more fury of the gale,
Feel through the cracks of my sepulchral vault
The fine-drawn probe of air, and watch the pale
Unearthly lightnings leap across the sky
Like sudden sperm and die and leap again.
The thunder calls and every spasm of fire
Beckons, a signal, to that old desire
In calm for tempest and at ease for pain.
Dreaming of strength and courage, here I lie.

MEDITERRANEAN

THIS tideless sapphire uniformly brims
Its jewelled circle of Tyrrhenian shore.
No vapours tarnish, not a cloud bedims,
And time descending only more and more
Makes rich, makes deep the unretiring gem.
And yet for me who look on it, how wide
The world of mud to which my thoughts con-
    demn
This loathing vision of a sunken tide!
The ebb is mine.   Life to its lowest neap
Withdrawn reveals that black and hideous shoal

I

Where I lie stranded.   Oh deliver me
From this defiling death!   Moon of the soul,
Call back the tide that ran so strong and deep,
Call back the shining jewel of the sea.

TIDE

AND if the tide should be for ever low,
The silted channels turned to ooze and mire?
And this grey delta—if it still should grow,
Bank after bank, and still the sea retire?
Retire beyond the halcyon hopes of noon
And silver night, the threat of wind and wave,
Past all the dark compulsion of the moon,
Past resurrection, past her power to save?
There is a firm consenting to disaster,
Proud resignation to accepted pain.
Pain quickens him who makes himself its master,
And quickening battle crowns both loss and gain.
But to this silting of the soul, who gives
Consent is no more man, no longer lives.

FÊTE NATIONALE

THESE lamps, like some miraculous gift of rain,
Evoke an April from the dusty weight
Of leaves that hang resigned and know their fate,
Expecting autumn: they are young again.
And young these dancers underneath the trees
Who pass and pass, how many all at one!

Like things of wax beneath an Indian sun,
Melted in music.   Oh, to be one of these,
Of these the born inhabitants of earth,
Each other's joyful captives!   Oh, to be
Safe home from these far islands, where the free,
Whose exile buys the honour of their birth,
Hark back across the liberating sea
To the lost continent of tears and mirth!

MIDSUMMER DAY

THIS day was midsummer, the longest tarrying
Time makes between two sleeps.   What have I done
With this longest of so few days, how spent,
Dear God, the golden, golden gift of sun?
Virginal, when I rose, the morning lay
Ready for beauty's rape, for wisdom's marrying.
I wrote: only an inky spider went,
Smear after smear, across the unsullied day.
If there were other places, if there were
But other days than this longest of few;
If one had courage, did one dare to do
That which alone might kill what now defaces
This the one place of all the countless places,
This only day when one will never dare!

AUTUMN STILLNESS

GREY is the air and silent as the sea's
Abysmal calm.   One solitary bird
Calls from far time and other boughs than these;

Oh, bright sad woods and melancholy sky,
Is there no cure for beauty but to run
Yet faster as faster flee hours, flowers and doxies
And dying music, until we also die?

ARMOUR

CRABS in their shells, because they cannot play
Don Juan or the flageolet, are safe;
And every stout Sir Roger, stout Sir Ralph,
Every Black Prince, Bayard and Bourchier may
(Their ribs and rumps hermetically canned)
Securely laugh at arrow, sword and mace.
But in their polished and annealed embrace,
Beneath their iron kiss and iron hand,
The soft defenceless lips and flowery breast,
The tender, tender belly of love receive
From helm and clasping cop and urgent greave
So deep a bruise that, mortally possessed,
Love dies.   Only the vulnerable will
Holds what it takes and, holding, does not kill.

SHEEP

SEEING a country churchyard, when the grey
Monuments walked, I with a second glance,
Doubting, postponed the apparent judgment day
To watch instead the random slow advance

Across the down of a hundred nibbling sheep.
And yet these tombs, half fancied and half seen
In the dim world between waking and sleep,
These headstones browsing on their plot of green,
Were sheep indeed and emblems of all life.
For man to dust, dust turns to grass, and grass
Grows wool and feeds on grass. The butcher's
    knife
Works magic, and the ephemeral sheep forms pass
Through swift tombs and through silent tombs,
    until
Once more God's acre feeds across the hill.

BLACK COUNTRY

Count yourselves happy that you are not rewarded
For your deserts with brimstone from on high.
Mean, mean among the slag-heaps, mean and sordid,
Your smoking town proclaims its blasphemy.
And yet, too merciful, the offended light
Forgives not only, but with vesperal gold
And roses of the sun repays your spite.
Shining transfigured in the Northern cold,
Instead of chimneys rise Italian towers,
While temples at their feet, not factories, shine;
And like the yet unbodied dream of flowers
Hangs the flushed smoke, through which these eyes
    divine
Enormous gestures of the gods' fierce wooing,
The nacreous flights, the limbs of bronze pursuing.

CARPE NOCTEM

THERE is no future, there is no more past,
No roots nor fruits, but momentary flowers.
Lie still, only lie still and night will last,
Silent and dark, not for a space of hours,
But everlastingly.   Let me forget
All but your perfume, every night but this,
The shame, the fruitless weeping, the regret.
Only lie still: this faint and quiet bliss
Shall flower upon the brink of sleep and spread,
Till there is nothing else but you and I
Clasped in a timeless silence.   But like one
Who, doomed to die, at morning will be dead,
I know, though night seem dateless, that the sky
Must brighten soon before to-morrow's sun.

THE PERGOLA

PILLARS, round which the wooden serpents clamber
Towards their own leaves, support the emerald shade,
The eyes, the amethysts, the clustered amber,
That weave the ceiling of this colonnade.
How many thousand Tyrrhenian Septembers
Muskily ripen in a sun-warmed skin!
With all my autumns.   For this tongue remembers
Grapes that made sweet a sick child's medicine,
Grapes of the South and of the submarine
Dusk of an English hot-house.   But when night
Lids every shining glance of sky between

Leaves now extinct, groping, bereft of sight,
I reach for grapes, but from an inward vine
Pluck sea-cold nipples, still bedewed with brine.

LINES

ALL day the wheels turn;
All day long the roaring of wheels, the rasping
Weave their imprisoning lattices of noise,
And hammers, hammers in the substance of the world
Carve out another cavernous world, a narrow
Sepulchre, and seal it from the sky,
Lord, with how great a stone!

Only a little beyond the factory walls
Silence is a flawless bowl of crystal,
Brimming, brimming with who can say beforehand,
Who can, returning, even remember what
Beautiful secret.   Only a little beyond
These hateful walls the birds among the branches
Secretly come and go.

Time also sleeps, but on the darkening threshold
Of each eternity pauses a moment
And still is time, but empty; still is time,
And therefore knows his emptiness.
The walls are crumbled, the stone is rolled away
(Is there one within? is there a resurrection?);
Stars through the ruined lattices bear witness,
Bear shining witness to the further silence,
Witness to the night.

Night is pregnant; silence, alive with voices;
The fullness of the tomb is but corruption;
Only the lifted stone invites the messengers,
Only the empty sepulchre, and only
Now and then, evokes
That which from the sepulchre arises.

Shy strangers, visiting feet came softly treading,
Came very softly sometimes in the darkness,
Oh, of what far nights and distant tombs!
Came suddenly into the empty time,
Came secretly and lingered secretly,
And through the unsealed door
Beckoned me on to follow.

I have made time empty again; empty, it invites
    them;
They do not come; have rolled away the stone,
But lie unrisen, lie unvisited.
Merciful God, bid them to come again!
Sometimes in winter
Sea-birds follow the plough,
And the bare field is all alive with wings,
With their white wings and unafraid alightings,
Sometimes in winter. And will they come again?

THE CICADAS

SIGHTLESS, I breathe and touch; this night of pines
Is needly, resinous and rough with bark.
Through every crevice in the tangible dark
The moonlessness above it all but shines.

Limp hangs the leafy sky; never a breeze
Stirs, nor a foot in all this sleeping ground;
And there is silence underneath the trees—
The living silence of continuous sound.

For like inveterate remorse, like shrill
Delirium throbbing in the fevered brain,
An unseen people of cicadas fill
Night with their one harsh note, again, again.

Again, again, with what insensate zest!
What fury of persistence, hour by hour!
Filled with what devil that denies them rest,
Drunk with what source of pleasure and of power!

Life is their madness, life that all night long
Bids them to sing and sing, they know not why;
Mad cause and senseless burden of their song;
For life commands, and Life! is all their cry.

I hear them sing, who in the double night
Of clouds and branches fancied that I went
Through my own spirit's dark discouragement,
Deprived of inward as of outward sight:

Who, seeking, even as here in the wild wood,
A lamp to beckon through my tangled fate,
Found only darkness and, disconsolate,
Mourned the lost purpose and the vanished good.

Now in my empty heart the crickets' shout
Re-echoing denies and still denies
With stubborn folly all my learned doubt,
In madness more than I in reason wise.

Life, life! The word is magical. They sing,
And in my darkened soul the great sun shines;
My fancy blossoms with remembered spring,
And all my autumns ripen on the vines.

Life! and each knuckle of the fig-tree's pale
Dead skeleton breaks out with emerald fire.
Life! and the tulips blow, the nightingale
Calls back the rose, calls back the old desire:

And old desire that is for ever new,
Desire, life's earliest and latest birth,
Life's instrument to suffer and to do,
Springs with the roses from the teeming earth;

Desire that from the world's bright body strips
Deforming time and makes each kiss the first;
That gives to hearts, to satiated lips
The endless bounty of to-morrow's thirst.

Time passes, and the watery moonrise peers
Between the tree-trunks. But no outer light
Tempers the chances of our groping years,
No moon beyond our labyrinthine night.

Clueless we go; but I have heard thy voice,
Divine Unreason! harping in the leaves,
And grieve no more; for wisdom never grieves,
And thou hast taught me wisdom; I rejoice.

THE WORLD OF LIGHT
A COMEDY IN THREE ACTS

This play was first produced by Mr. Leon M. Lion at the Royalty Theatre, London, on March 30, 1931, with the following cast:

Mrs. Wenham	MARGARET HALSTAN
Mr. Wenham	AUBREY MATHER
Hugo Wenham	DENYS BLAKELOCK
Enid Deckle	FABIA DRAKE
Maid	AILEEN WOOD
Bill Hamblin	SEBASTIAN SHAW
Hubert Capes	PHILIP BRANDON
Mr. Gray	MARCUS BARRON

THE WORLD OF LIGHT

ACT I

SCENE I

The drawing-room in the Wenhams' house in the country.

> (MR. WENHAM *is sitting in front of the fire reading.* MRS. WENHAM *is writing letters. Silence for some seconds after the rise of the curtain.*)

MRS. WENHAM (*she is a woman of about thirty-five, handsome, large, commanding*). John dear. (*He looks up from his book.*) What's the time?

MR. WENHAM (*he is twenty-five years older than his wife, a well-preserved man, nice-looking in a grey suppressed way. His manner is very gentle*). Twenty to seven, dear.

MRS. WENHAM. I shall have to go and say good-night to the children in a moment.

MR. WENHAM. I'll come too. Whenever you give the word, my love.

MRS. WENHAM. As a matter of fact, John, I'd rather you didn't come up. I'd like you to say a few words to Hugo when he arrives. About Enid.

MR. WENHAM (*nervously*). But, my dear, wouldn't it be better if you . . . I mean, a woman's touch . . . in these delicate matters . . .

MRS. WENHAM. One would think you were afraid of him, John. Afraid of your own son.

MR. WENHAM. No, no, my dear. It's not that.

But one has a certain . . . a certain diffidence. Besides, I'm not very good at this sort of thing . . . I mean, discussing . . . well, shall we say, the affairs of the heart. So wouldn't it be better if you were to talk to him?

MRS. WENHAM (*firmly*). No, John, I'm afraid it must be you. After all, I'm only his stepmother, I can't speak to him as you can speak. And then, in the second place, I'm a woman, I'm a friend of Enid's. If I spoke to him, he might feel that it was a kind of feminine conspiracy to get him married, which would spoil everything. Because I *do* want him to get married. I really think it would be the making of him. Besides, there's *her* point of view to be considered. You see, it's really not fair on her. This friendship that's gone on ever since they were children and never quite turns into something else. Always on the brink. It's not fair. Don't you agree with me, John?

MR. WENHAM. Oh, quite, quite.

MRS. WENHAM. She has a right to expect Hugo to marry her. After all, she's nearly thirty, and I know for a fact that she's refused at least two other men. So you see, John, something ought to be done about it.

MR. WENHAM. Yes, I quite agree, my dear.

MRS. WENHAM. Hugo's been getting so unsettled recently. I don't like it. It's high time he got married. Besides, he's really rather a helpless person. He needs looking after. Enid would mother him. They *ought* to marry. Hugo's making quite a reasonable income now at Cambridge. Besides, Enid has three or four hundred of her own. And if necessary, you could always give him a little.

MR. WENHAM. Oh, one had always meant to, when Hugo . . . well, embarked on matrimony.

MRS. WENHAM. So you see there's no reason why they shouldn't get married. And a great many reasons why they should. As soon as possible. And that's what I want you to say to Hugo when he comes.

MR. WENHAM. Yes, dear. All the same, I do wish you could stay and help one to . . . explain it to him.

MRS. WENHAM. Out of the question, John.

MR. WENHAM. One's so loath to break in on a young man's . . . well, should one say his emotional privacies ? . . .

MRS. WENHAM. There ! I hear the car. Remember, John. I rely on you.

MR. WENHAM (*agitated*). Yes, dear. But really, it seems to me . . .

MRS. WENHAM. And say what you have to say as quickly as possible, dear. Because, you see, I arranged that Enid should come rather early, so that there'd be a chance of her being alone with Hugo, before dinner. So don't be too slow. And when Enid comes, just slip away. Tactfully, you know. Inconspicuously.

MR. WENHAM. Yes, but . . .

MRS. WENHAM. Say you've got to say good-night to the children.

> (*Enter* HUGO WENHAM. *He is a man of about thirty, small, rather delicate-looking, with an ugly, but sensitive, intelligent face, and a manner whose timidity is tempered by sudden spurts of brusque determination.*)

Ah, Hugo ! This is nice to see you. (*Holds out her hand.*) But you're icy. Come near the fire.

K

HUGO.   Thank you.   How are you, father?

MR. WENHAM.   As flourishing as can be expected.
And you, dear boy?

HUGO.   Oh, all right.   Rather tired, of course.   But
at the end of term one always is.   Trying to make
reluctant undergraduates understand Plato—
God! (*He shakes his head.   To* MRS. WENHAM)
How are the children, Alice?

MRS. WENHAM.   Very well, thanks.   Peter's been
having a bit of a sore throat.   That's all.   Which
reminds me, I must go and say good-night to
them.   I'll leave you.   Dinner's at half-past
seven.   Don't dress.

HUGO.   Oh, talking of dinner, I hope you didn't
mind my asking Bill Hamblin for this evening.

MRS. WENHAM.   But we're delighted.

HUGO.   He's leaving England to-morrow.   It was
my only chance of seeing him before he started.
I hope you'll like him.

MRS. WENHAM.   I'm sure we shall.

HUGO.   Don't be *too* sure.   But anyhow, you'll be
amused, I think.   I find him a real tonic (*laughs*),
and after a spell of Cambridge one needs a tonic,
I assure you.

MRS. WENHAM.   He sounds charming.   And as I
wrote to you, I've asked Enid to drop in too.   So
it ought to be a delightful evening.   But I must
fly. (*She goes out.*)
    (*Pause.*)

MR. WENHAM.   Well, dear boy, it's pleasant to have
you with us again.

HUGO.   It's pleasant to be here. (*Another embarrassed pause.*)   Been very busy lately, father?

MR. WENHAM.   Oh, the daily round, the common
task.

HUGO.   Yes, if only they could be a bit more irregular and extraordinary.

MR. WENHAM.   I used to wish the same at your age. But one settles down; one gets to like the harness; one comes to realise that the daily and the common are . . . are sacred.

HUGO.   Sacred ? (*Makes a little grimace.*) I'd like to be able to feel that.

MR. WENHAM.   Not the only sacred, of course. There's the other—the sublimer aspect of sacredness. (*He sighs.*) I wish I could persuade you to take more interest in spiritualism, dear boy.

HUGO.   But I do.   I read all the documents.

MR. WENHAM.   Yes, but in what sort of spirit ? Not as they ought to be read.   You're detached. If you only knew how . . . how consoling and uplifting it was.

HUGO.   I don't know that I awfully want to be consoled and uplifted. (*He begins walking up and down the room.*)   And anyhow, if the common and the daily weren't so dismal, would one need all that consolation ?   I mean, couldn't one's whole life be made sacred in that sublimer, more exciting way ?   Here and now, without calling in the next world to redress the balance of this.   The infinite in terms of the bounded and the relative— that's what I try to see my way towards.   Gropingly. (*He breaks off to utter a constrained little laugh.*)   Sorry I'm being a bit of a bore.

MR. WENHAM.   But, no, dear boy. (*He lays a hand on his arm shyly.*)   One's so happy to be allowed to . . . to share your thoughts.   So happy and so . . . so proud.

HUGO (*very much embarrassed and trying to laugh it*

off).   Oh, there's not much to be proud of, I'm afraid.

MR. WENHAM.   One understands so well what you mean.   That raising of life to a higher . . . well, level of significance . . . one's felt the need of that oneself.   One has tried ; one has, perhaps, to some extent, succeeded.   (*A little pause.*) Listen, dear boy, I was wrong just now when I said that the common and the daily were sacred in themselves.   Rather they become sacred when they're . . . they're shared with . . . well, somebody one's attached to; when they're made the . . . the foundation and background of . . . well, of love. That's the real point of marriage—its power to enrich ordinariness and make it sacred.   Now, if you were to get married, dear boy . . .

HUGO (*laughing*).   Do you think I'd begin to enjoy trying to make stupid undergraduates understand Plato ?   No, but seriously, I have thought about it.

MR. WENHAM.   You have ?   That's good news.   (*He hesitates, nervously.*)   Very good news . . . because, you see, dear boy, one had been thinking about it so much oneself of late.   You and our dear Enid . . .

HUGO.   Enid ?

MR. WENHAM.   I mean, you've known her so long . . . such an intimate comradeship.   It was hard to think of any one more suitable, more . . . well, suitable.   And at the same time one hasn't been blind to the obvious fact that Enid herself is . . . well, devoted to you.

HUGO.   Is that obvious ?

MR. WENHAM.   But surely, Hugo, you yourself must have seen . . . well, what one was saying.

(HUGO *shakes his head slowly.*)

No? Well, to other eyes, it has been plain enough. (*Pause.*) Dear boy, I don't exactly know what your feelings are in this matter.

HUGO (*laughs*). I wish I exactly knew myself.

MR. WENHAM. It's often difficult to know before one's . . . one's acted on the knowledge.

HUGO. On the knowledge one hasn't got?

MR. WENHAM. But one assumes it. And one acts on the assumption. And the result of the action is to prove . . . well, that the assumption was correct.

HUGO. Or incorrect. What happens in that case?

MR. WENHAM. One's never seen it proved incorrect.

HUGO. You mean that pretending to be in love always makes you really be in love?

MR. WENHAM. Not *pretending*, dear boy. The cases one was talking about are cases . . . cases where the old habit of companionship seems to exclude the possibility of a new revelation. All one was saying is that if you take a risk and give the new revelation a chance . . . well, it does manifest itself, in spite of the old habit. Always.

HUGO. All the same, there might be exceptions.

MR. WENHAM. And then, dear boy, there's Enid to be thought about. Would it be really . . . well, just to . . . to . . . I mean, *not* to marry her? (*Hastily, very embarrassed*) I mean if it were possible for you to marry her—possible as far as your own feelings went. Would it really be quite the . . . quite the . . . well, chivalrous thing?

HUGO. Chivalrous? But where have I been unchivalrous? Do you mean to imply . . . ?

MR. WENHAM. No, no, dear boy. One wasn't implying anything. Only there's this to be thought: that an old friendship like yours, a friendship with a woman, and a woman who's . . . who's . . . well, devoted to you, well, it . . . it automatically gives the friend to understand that . . . that she's more than a friend.

HUGO. But do you mean to say that Enid thinks . . . ? I mean, does she feel I've not been treating her fairly ?

MR. WENHAM. Oh, no, she never says anything, of course not. All that one meant was that her present situation was—how shall I say it ?—was in itself a kind of . . . of protest.

HUGO. You mean her life looks as though it had been spoilt ?

MR. WENHAM. No, no. Hardly that. But it seems to me that it might come to be spoilt.

HUGO. If I didn't marry her ?

MR. WENHAM. You or some one else. And one knows privately that she's refused several other offers of marriage.

HUGO. She never told me that.

MR. WENHAM. Of course she didn't. Do you think it would be like Enid to . . . to do anything that might look like . . . well, forcing your hand ? But all the same, one happens to know from other sources that it's true. And the reason for it . . . well, dear boy, the reason is *you*. So that you see, in a way it's not quite fair to let things go on as they are. The right, the chivalrous thing to do would be either to stop seeing her altogether— that is, if you felt it was impossible to . . . well, feel more than friendship . . . or else . . .

HUGO. Yes, yes, I see. (*Pause.*)

MR. WENHAM. I think you ought to come to a decision, Hugo. (*The door opens and* ENID *enters quietly.*) You ought to make up your mind.

ENID (*she is a dark woman about twenty-eight, with large eyes and an emotional, intense expression*). Do you think Hugo can ever make up his mind ?
(*The two men start and look round guiltily.*)
Oh, I'm sorry to have given you such a start. Good evening, Mr. Wenham. Well, Hugo ?
(*They shake hands in silence.*)
(*Turning to* MR. WENHAM) What were you telling him to make up his mind about ?

MR. WENHAM. Oh, nothing, my dear, nothing.

ENID. Those are the decisions he finds hardest to make. The ones about nothing. How I've suffered from his not knowing what restaurant he wants to go to for lunch, and when at last he does get somewhere, not being able to decide between the roast chicken and the veal cutlet. Terrible ! Isn't it true, Hugo ?

HUGO (*gloomily*). I suppose so.

ENID. To eat roast chicken or not to eat roast chicken, that is the question. But *I'm* like Lady Macbeth. Infirm of purpose, give *me* the menu. Poor old Hugo !

HUGO. Poor old everybody, it seems.

MR. WENHAM (*looking at his watch*). Oh, dear ! One must be running up to say good-night to the children. I shall get into trouble if I'm late.
(*He goes out.*)

ENID (*going up to* HUGO *and examining him critically*). You look tired, Hugo.

HUGO. Mayn't I be tired ? And anyhow, you needn't throw it in my teeth.

ENID. I was only throwing a little sympathy. You generally like it. Besides, you *do* look tired. A tonic—that's what you need. I'll get you a bottle of hypophosphates to-morrow.

HUGO (*with a kind of weary impatience*). No, don't. Please.

ENID (*playfully*). Yes, I will. And I'll stand over you to see that you take it.

(HUGO *says nothing, but his face shows that this spritely talk of tonics distresses him.*)

But what's the matter, Hugo?

HUGO. Nothing!

ENID. It must be a nasty sort of nothing. How's life?

HUGO (*shrugging his shoulders*). Oh, as usual. Rather like death.

ENID. I hate it when you say that sort of thing.

HUGO. I'm sorry. Would you like me to say that every day in every way it's getting better and better?

(ENID *says nothing.*)

What have you been up to since I saw you last? Bullying the deserving poor, as usual?

ENID. Yes, my old Charity Organisation business. And parcels of books from Mudie's in the intervals.

HUGO. Bad novels to counteract the good works— I know. And then early service on Sunday morning, and 'Abide with me, fast falls the eventide,' on Sunday evening.

ENID. Which you needn't laugh at, Hugo.

HUGO. Oh, I don't. On the contrary. I wish *I* were a theolater.

ENID. A what?

HUGO. A theolater. A man who worships God.

ENID. How does any one contrive not to? God's there—it's so obvious.

HUGO. Yes, obvious, I know.

ENID. Then why?

HUGO. Because just knowing isn't any good. (*He*

laughs.) I know I'm a man, for example; but that doesn't prevent me from often feeling a worm.

ENID. Which is just stupid, Hugo. You take a pleasure in feeling a worm. It's really rather disgusting.

HUGO. Yes, you're quite right. Disgusting. But then I do so enjoy being sorry for myself. It's a vice—something one hates and at the same time feels irresistibly attracted to. . . . Don't you ever feel sorry for yourself, Enid?

ENID. Oh, sometimes. But who doesn't?

HUGO. Well, what do you think about it?

ENID. Try to think about something else.

HUGO. God, for example? That's where theolatry must come in so useful. But that smell of a congregation on a wet Sunday morning—I wish *I* could feel it was the odour of sanctity. But, no. . . . (*He shakes his head*.) I really prefer the smell of cows. And then the service—so far as I'm concerned, the divinity it's addressed to is dead, stone-dead. If only I could find a live one.

ENID. You would if you looked.

HUGO (*he shakes his head*). Only a live man can find a live god. And when one's dead, as I am . . . There you are! Being sorry for myself again. But it happens to be true. I'm dead, I'm empty. A dead vacuum. How I'm enjoying this. And how you're hating it, Enid!

ENID. It just makes me feel miserable—miserable for your sake.

HUGO. Thank you. But I hope you also feel contemptuous. (*She shakes her head*.) No? Well, you ought to. (*Pause*.) I heard Mozart's G minor quintet last week. That's very nearly a living god—I mean, music like that.

ENID (*nodding and in a seriously ecstatic voice*). Yes, great music. . . .

HUGO (*made suddenly flippant by her earnestness*). And then what about great alcohol ? I got absurdly tight when I was staying one week-end with Bill Hamblin. Perhaps champagne 's another of the living gods. If only one could be permanently buffy ! Bill Hamblin 's in that state even when he 's perfectly sober. Bubblingly alive and therefore surrounded by a whole pantheon of living gods. I envy him.

ENID. Do you think I 'll like Bill Hamblin ?

HUGO. You 'll probably fall in love with him. Most women do.

ENID (*smiling sadly*). I 'm afraid that 's not very likely.

HUGO. Don't you be too sure. (*Pause.*) What about this love business, now ? Is love also a dead god ?

ENID. He 's got to be born before he can die. You 'd better first ask yourself if he 's been born.

HUGO. I do, constantly. But I don't get any answer. But do you think he 's got to be like the poets, *born* ? I mean, can't he also be *made* ? What do you think, Enid ? Can love be made ?

ENID. There 'd have to be the makings first. Nothing can be made unless the makings are there first.

HUGO. And what are they ? Affection, understanding, common tastes, a shared history— would you call those the makings of love ?

ENID. I suppose so. But why do you ask me ?

HUGO. What a stupid hypocritical question, Enid ! You know quite well why I asked you.

ENID. I don't. But still . . .

HUGO. Well, if you don't, I may as well go on leaving you in the dark. (*Pause ; he walks up and down, then at last, with the air of a man who has taken a decision, halts in front of her.*) Look here, Enid ; suppose I were to say to you that I didn't love you, but that I had all the makings of love in me. And suppose that on the strength of those makings I were to ask you to marry me— which would be asking you to marry a dead man, but a dead man with a chance of coming to life, if he could love. Suppose all this ; would you take a risk and try whether love and life could be made out of those makings, or else, if it couldn't be made —well, God knows what would happen if it couldn't be made. Would you take that risk, Enid ?

ENID (*after a pause*). Would *you* take it, Hugo ?

HUGO. I ? It depends on how you feel about it.

ENID. Which depends on what *you* feel.

HUGO. No, I want to know what *your* feelings are.

ENID (*laughing and shaking her head*). Oh, Hugo, Hugo.

HUGO. No, don't laugh, Enid. Why do you laugh ?

ENID. All this depending on other dependings. Why can't you make up your mind ? It's the old story of the roast chicken and the veal cutlet.

HUGO (*hurt*). Well, if that's how you feel, I won't go on. I had an idea you cared. Otherwise I wouldn't . . . (*He is turning to walk away, when she catches his hand and kisses it.*)

ENID. Hugo ! Don't be hurt. *Please.* (*Pause ; they look at one another, after a moment his eyes flinch away from hers embarrassed.*) Oh, if you only knew, Hugo. How much, how much . . . (*Kisses his hand again ; when she goes on speak-*

ing she keeps it pressed against her cheek.)   But I didn't want to tell you how much I cared.   Not before you 'd made up your mind.   It would have been bullying you, bludgeoning you with my love. (*She laughs unsteadily.*)   I don't want to be Lady Macbeth about *this*.   When it 's a question of chicken or veal cutlets, then it 's all right my saying ' Give *me* the daggers.'   But here—here you 've got to decide.   This is your risk.   Where there 's love there isn't any risk.   Or at least the reward is so great, that the risk doesn't count. But there, I 'm bullying you.   I 'm bludgeoning you with my feelings.   Go, go. (*She pushes him away from her.*)   Forget what I said.   Don't be influenced by it. (*He moves back towards her ; she pushes him away again.*)   No, go.   You must make up your mind at the other end of the room. Go.

>   (HUGO *stands hesitatingly for a few seconds, sheepishly, then moves away.   The door opens.*)

MAID.   Mr. Hamblin.

>   (*Enter* BILL HAMBLIN.   *He is a young man of about* HUGO'S *age, thin, with an aquiline face and pale, silky hair.   The skin is tanned till it is almost darker than the hair.   The eyes are a very bright blue.   His movements are quick and dancing.   There is something gay and irresponsible about him, though he were not quite human, a sort of fairy.*)

BILL.   Well, Hugo, what fun to see you !   Escaped from your ghastly academic prison ?   But you don't look as cheerful about it as I should have expected.   Glum, boy, glum. (*Seeing* ENID) But I 'm so sorry.   Why didn't you introduce me, Hugo ?

HUGO. You didn't give me time ; Enid, this is Bill
   Hamblin. Miss Enid Deckle.

ENID (*as she shakes his hand*). I've heard so much
   about you from Hugo.

BILL. And yet you still shake me by the hand.
   You're discreet, Hugo, thank you. So am I,
   though. Not that there's any need for discretion
   in this case, Miss Deckle. Hugo's an absolute
   monster of honesty and temperance and chastity.

HUGO (*laughing*). Alas !

BILL. I've done my best for him. But it's no good.
   He's incorrigibly the good citizen. It's dis-
   couraging. What a charming dress you're wearing, if you'll allow me to say so.

ENID. I'm glad you like it.

BILL. Really ravishing. Don't you think so, Hugo ?

HUGO. Well, now you mention it . . . As a matter
   of fact, I hadn't noticed.

ENID (*laughing*). Hugo never notices anything.

BILL. I know. These budding professors—they're
   above all that sort of thing. Or below it. But
   you should just listen to them chattering away
   together about the latest fashion in metaphysics.
   I hear that the Absolute is being worn rather short
   this year. Hugo, is that true ?

HUGO. On the contrary, it's been lengthened.

BILL. Well, thank God for that. I was getting
   rather tired of these pragmatist fashions. I like
   my universe well draped with transcendental mysteries. Layers and layers of mystery, like petti-
   coats. White mystery, black mystery. Have you
   ever been in a tropical forest, Miss Deckle ?

ENID. Never.

BILL. Ah, you should go. Talk of black mysteries
   —it's like a cellar, like the crypt of a church—the

devil's own cathedral. Nobody has a sufficient respect for the devil in our civilised temperate countries. You have to go to the tropics to see him functioning on the grand scale. The forests of Borneo, for example. Marvellous! Satan in all his grandeur. I went there an agnostic, but they converted me: I came back a convinced devil worshipper. I'm always telling Hugo that he ought to come to the tropics with me. No philosophy has ever been written in the jungle. And everything that's been written out of the jungle is just nonsense under the trees in the hothouse darkness. What an opportunity for somebody who wants to say something *new*! But Hugo prefers his rooms in Trinity. Well, well, there's no accounting for tastes. Particularly perverted tastes. Because, you know, he really hates being at Cambridge.

ENID. He only imagines he hates it. He'd be much wretcheder anywhere else.

BILL. What a man! Aren't you ashamed of yourself, Hugo?

HUGO. Why should I be?

BILL. For being unhappy. It's criminal, it's a vice. By the way, talking of vice, did I tell you that I'd bought a light amphibian?

HUGO. A what?

BILL. An amphibian. A seaplane that's also got wheels, so that you can come down on earth or water, which you like. Lovely little machine. I'm taking it with me to Guiana.

ENID. Are you going to Guiana, Mr. Hamblin?
　　(*As she speaks, enter* MR. *and* MRS. WENHAM.)

BILL. To-morrow morning, to be precise.

HUGO (*taking* BILL *by the arm and leading him for-*

ward). Alice, this is Bill Hamblin. (*They shake hands.*) And my father.

BILL. How do you do, sir.

MR. WENHAM. How do you do. One's heard so much from Hugo . . .

BILL. Who's luckily so discreet, as I was saying to Miss Deckle.

MR. WENHAM. I hope we shall often have the pleasure of welcoming you here.

BILL. If and whenever I get back from Guiana.

(*Enter* MAID.)

ENID. Mr. Hamblin is taking an aeroplane with him.

MAID. Dinner is served.

MR. WENHAM. An aeroplane? You don't say so. How extremely . . .

MRS. WENHAM. Shall we go in to dinner? Come along, Enid.

(*They go out.*)

Curtain

SCENE II

A few seconds of darkness represents the lapse of three and a half hours.

(*The curtain rises again.* MR. *and* MRS. WENHAM *and* BILL *are sitting round the fire.*)

BILL (*politely*). You don't say so!

MR. WENHAM (*with triumph*). Ah, but that doesn't by any means exhaust the list of improvements. The art of accountancy is in full development. Consider ledger posting, for example. My firm now manufacture a machine for posting ledgers.

One mechanical operation posts to a ledger account, adds up and works out the balance on the account, makes out the monthly statement, and at the same time records the total of all the items posted, so that . . .

MRS. WENHAM. Dear, I think I'll be going up to bed. I hope you'll excuse me, Mr. Hamblin, if I say good-night.

BILL. Good-night, Mrs. Wenham. (*They shake hands.*) And thank you so much for your charming hospitality.

MRS. WENHAM. Hugo ought to be back in quite a few minutes now. I'm sorry he should have been dragged away from you like this. But you'll understand, some one had to see Enid home. John, don't forget to offer Mr. Hamblin some whisky. Good-night, once more, Mr. Hamblin.

BILL. Good-night.

(*She goes out.*)

MR. WENHAM (*moving to the table on which stand the bottles and glasses*). A little of the . . . (*playfully*) the blood of John Barleycorn?

BILL. The what? Oh, whisky. Yes, I'd love a drop of whisky.

MR. WENHAM. Will you say when—I believe that's the correct expression. Or it used to be.

BILL. Still is—absolutely correct. When, when, when! (*He takes the glass and fills it up from the syphon.*) There's been regrettably little progress in the art of drinking, I'm afraid. Not like accountancy. But I'm sorry to see that you're not joining me.

MR. WENHAM. No. One has always found that one . . . one flourished just as well without alcohol as with.

BILL.   You made the experiment?

MR. WENHAM.   Once, with some cider.   When I was quite a young man.   But one found it didn't agree with one.   And besides, one didn't even like it.

BILL.   I'm not surprised.   But did you never try anything else?

MR. WENHAM.   Never.   (*After a little pause he adds, hastily, afraid of having said something to embarrass his guest*)   Not that one has any objection to other people partaking . . . I mean, in moderation.

BILL.   Oh, in moderation, of course.   I've often wondered if there isn't such a thing as an excess of moderation.

MR. WENHAM.   I beg your pardon.

BILL.   Oh, nothing.   (*In another tone*)   Hugo tells me that you take an interest in psychical research, Mr. Wenham.   Is that true?

MR. WENHAM.   A very deep interest.

BILL.   And you've never travelled, have you?   I mean, out of Europe.

MR. WENHAM.   Alas, travel has been one of the luxuries one couldn't permit oneself.

BILL.   Well, it's a pity if you're interested in the supernormal.   I remember one time, for example, when I was with some howling dervishes near Ispahan . . .

MR. WENHAM.   Ah, but you evidently approach the subject from the . . . how shall I say? . . . the ethnological position.   I look at it from quite another standpoint.   One regards spiritualism as the . . . the highest form of contemporary religion.

BILL.   You think so?

MR. WENHAM.   The highest because the most

L

MR. WENHAM (*laying his hand on* HUGO'S *shoulder*).
Good-night, dear boy. (*He goes out.*)

HUGO. I hope you weren't too bored by the paternal
conversation.

BILL. On the contrary, I was charmed. One's too
apologetic for fathers nowadays, though of course
it is painfully obvious that you can't really hold
any communication with any one over sixty.
Strange, the way elderly people simply don't
understand certain things. Psychological things,
especially. How little they seem to realise
motives—their own or any one else's. It's what
comes of having been brought up before the dis-
covery of the unconscious—when man was still a
rational animal. Very queer. It's like talking
to some specially foreign kind of foreigner. But
there's a kind of innocence about them that's
charming. And then how they work! Like ants!
It's they who keep the world from collapsing.

HUGO. I sometimes wish it would collapse.

BILL. I don't. I like being free. You need a good
strong social framework to be free inside—a
framework of fathers all busily balancing accounts
and doing their duty, in order that a few ne'er-do-
weels like me can live in irresponsible freedom.
No, I'm most grateful to your father and the
other vertebrae in the social backbone. Grateful
and, my God! sorry for them. It's not much fun
being a vertebra.

HUGO. Don't tell *me* that. I'm a vertebra myself.

BILL. And on top of everything he's getting old,
your poor father. He was saying something just
as you came in—you interrupted him—something
that made me shudder. We'd been talking about
spiritualism.

HUGO. But I thought you'd been talking about accountancy?

BILL. Oh, we had. But the one led on to the other. Just as in your father's life. Led on inevitably. You can't specialise in accountancy without turning to some sort of compensation. And as he doesn't drink, it almost had to be spiritualism.

HUGO. Yes ; that and marriage. I told you he'd been married three times, didn't I ? My mother was his second wife.

BILL. Three times ? Well, well. Another whisky? (*He holds up the bottle.*)

HUGO. Thanks.

(BILL *fills up his glass and afterwards his own.*)

BILL. Well, we'd been talking about spiritualism, and I'd said what I've always thought about these matters : let the dead bury their dead. Because even if it *is* all true, which I'm quite prepared to believe, well, what of it ? It's the same with most of the facts of science. This chair— it's really a swarm of electrons whizzing about in a vacuum. But what of it ? For all practical purposes of life it's got to be a solid chair. And so with souls. Souls may be really detachable like . . . like chintz covers . . . they may go on existing after we're dead. All right. But again, what of it ? So let the dead bury their dead, and the electrons bury their electrons. I'm alive, and this thing I've got my bottom on is a chair.

HUGO. Well, as a professional metaphysician you can hardly expect me to agree with you there.

BILL. No, of course. But as a human being . . .

HUGO. I say, hear, hear ! And as one of the dead I say we ought to be buried.

BILL. Well, when I said that to your father, do you

know what he answered ? ' Jesus was a young man when he said, " Let the dead bury their dead." It 's easy to feel like that when you 're young, but at *my* age . . .' And then you came in. He didn't go on. But he 'd said enough to make the whole horror of growing old rise before me. Because when you 're old, you obviously just can't let the dead bury their dead. I 've never thought of that before. There are so many dead in an old man's universe, that he simply can't help thinking about them. Indeed, for a very old man, there are no living people at all. Every single one of the inhabitants of his world has gone. He 's left with nothing, alone. You can't expect *him* to go about saying, ' Let the dead bury their dead.' Oh, it 's a bad business this growing old.

HUGO. What do you propose to do about it ?

BILL. What can one do, except make the best of one's youth. (*Turning on* HUGO *with sudden fierceness.*) Not make the worst of it like you. You know, Hugo, you 're really intolerable. Sitting there at Cambridge enjoying your misery. It 's disgusting. Why don't you throw it all up and come with me to-morrow ?

HUGO. Well, to begin with, I simply haven't got the courage. After all, the job at Cambridge does mean a settled future.

BILL. But what sort of future ? Just as awful as the past.

HUGO. But settled, at any rate. Absolutely settled.

BILL. Settled dreariness. You 're a queer devil, Hugo ! Deliberately choosing dreariness.

HUGO. Yes, but don't forget that in return for the dreariness I 've got the certainty of never going hungry, of always being respectable . . .

BILL.   Christ!

HUGO.   Of always being able to afford to be honest.
   Of never having to commit a crime.

BILL.   Not to mention never having to be a man.

HUGO (*after a little pause*).   I suppose I'm a born
   coward?

BILL.   Born?   No.   Made.

HUGO (*laughs*).   Like love, eh?

BILL.   Like what?

HUGO.   Oh, nothing.

BILL.   No, no, it's your education that's respon-
   sible.   Thank God, I never had anything to do
   with respectable people.   You've no idea what
   an advantage it is to be brought up by a jolly
   drunken spendthrift like my father.

HUGO.   Not to mention the advantage of being born
   an aristocrat, with money in the background,
   generations of unearned increment.

BILL (*laughing*).   My father got rid of most of that
   all right.

HUGO.   Yes, but not all.   And anyhow, the tradition
   of money persisted.   Caste and money—between
   them they put a man above public opinion.
   Almost above fate—above all the fate, anyhow,
   that's embodied in society.   You don't care about
   what the lower animals think.   Well, when
   you're an aristocrat and rich, that's what the
   public is—a collection of lower animals; and
   public opinion is just a huge noise of mooing and
   bleating.

BILL (*laughing*).   Not to mention grunting and
   braying, and howling and gibbering.   But after
   all, you needn't be an aristocrat to think that.
   It's what any sensible man thinks about public
   opinion.   It's what *you* think, for example.

HUGO.   Yes, with my head.   But the rest of me has a kind of abject respect for the braying and the gibbering.   Because, you see, the rest of me's bourgeois.   Born and brought up amongst the lower animals, *as* a lower animal; in a world where people simply can't afford not to conform and be respectable.   Playing for safety—that's what we lower animals are taught from the cradle. It becomes a second nature.   And when one's a bit of a coward to start with, as I'm afraid I am . . . (*He shrugs his shoulders.*)   Well, you understand why I am frightened of throwing up my job.

BILL (*holding out the bottle*).   Then you'd better take a little more Dutch courage.

HUGO.   No, really; I've had too much already.

BILL.   Nonsense.   Give me your glass.

    (HUGO *holds out his glass.*)

  You mustn't be like your father.

HUGO.   I'm afraid I *am* rather like him.

BILL.   Well, at any rate you've had enough imprudence to experiment with other things besides cider.   Was he angry with you when you decided not to be a teetotaller?

HUGO.   No, not angry.

BILL.   More in sorrow than in anger, I take it.

HUGO.   Oh, much more in sorrow.   *Only* in sorrow. My father's never angry.   That's one of his worst defects.   Even when I was a child—and I was insufferable—he never lost his temper with me . . . always restrained himself.   Yes, there was always restraint—in everything.   Why is it that good people are so awful?   I mean that sort of good people.   I'm afraid it's my fate to be good.

BILL.   Well, if you want it to be your fate, of course
   it will be.

HUGO.   But I don't want it to be.   God, how drunk
   you 've made me with all this whisky.   (*Empties
   his glass.*)   I absolutely don't want it to be.

BILL.   And yet you 're allowing it to become your
   fate.   You're just letting yourself drift.   And what
   makes it worse is that you know you 're drifting ;
   and worse still, that you like drifting, you want to
   destroy yourself.

HUGO (*suddenly laughing ;   he is rather tipsy*).   Did
   I ever tell you that my father wrote verses for the
   magazines ?

BILL.   No.

HUGO.   Secretly, under a pseudonym.   Oh, the
   greasiest sentiments !   and then a kind of arch
   playfulness.   It 's one of the penalties he pays
   for goodness, I suppose.   Like his spiritualism.
   Think of sentimentalising with the dead !

BILL.   You 'll be doing the same in a few years if
   you 're not careful.

HUGO.   No, no.   I shall take to writing children's
   stories.   Very charming and whimsical, you know.
   And I shall pinch little girls' legs in trains.
   (*Laughs extravagantly.*)   And one day I shall get
   into the clutches of the police—' Serious charge
   against professor.'   You can see the headlines.
   But all my friends will come and give evidence
   about my irreproachable morality.   And I shall
   leave the court without a stain on my character.
   Yes, absolutely without a stain.   Pure, my boy,
   pure.   Chemically pure.   *Du bist wie eine Blume,
   so hold und rein und schön.*   Yes, I shall leave the
   court without a stain, and immediately rush off to
   find another little girl to pinch.   And when I 've

pinched her I shall go home and write another
of my sweet little whimsical children's stories.
Much better than spiritualism, don't you think ?

BILL (*after a pause, quietly and seriously*). Why
don't you come with me to-morrow ?

HUGO. I 've told you.

BILL. Do you mean the question of courage ?   But
I tell you it 's not difficult to be courageous.   Or
at least it 's not difficult to be foolhardy, and that 's
all you 've got to be at the moment.   Just shut
your eyes and jump.   It 's nothing.   And afterwards what happens, happens.

HUGO.   But what happens to be happening to
me at the moment is that I 'm engaged to be
married.

BILL.   Since when ?

HUGO (*looking at his wrist-watch*).   Since about
eleven-twenty-two.

BILL.   You mean just now, with Miss What 's-her-
name ?

HUGO.   With Miss What 's-her-name, precisely.

BILL.   But I had no idea that you had any inten-
tion . . .

HUGO.   Nor had I till this evening.

BILL.   Or that you even . . . well, much cared.

HUGO (*laughing*).   I don't.   That 's just the point.
That 's just the beauty of it !

BILL.   Oh, God !   I give you up, Hugo.   You 're
really too awful.   I think I 'd better go home.
(*Rises from his chair.*)

HUGO (*pushing him down again*).   No, don't go,
Bill.   You mustn't go.   Have another drink, do.

BILL.   No, no, let me . . .

HUGO.   Just one more.   I beg you.   (*Takes* BILL'S
glass and fills it, then his own.)   The last drink

together, Bill. Drink, drink for ever, for ever
drink.

BILL. Oh, very well.

HUGO. The absolutely last. (*Raising his glass.*)
To your adventures, Bill. To the tropics.
Especially Capricorn, dear Capricorn, whom I
shall never, never see. (*Drinks.*)

BILL. What do you expect *me* to drink to? To
Cambridge? To metaphysics, to your pupils?

HUGO. Oh, all that, and my marriage. Bill, you 're
forgetting my marriage.

BILL. I wish I could forget it. As a matter of curiosity, Hugo—no, I 'm not going to bully you
about it—but just as a matter of curiosity, may I
ask you why?

HUGO. Why not, after all?

BILL. If you don't care.

HUGO. Well, I wanted to make sure that I didn't,
by experiment.

BILL. No, but seriously . . .

HUGO. Seriously, Bill, have you ever been blackmailed?

BILL (*shakes his head*). It 's one of the advantages
of not being afraid of public opinion.

HUGO. You needn't be. It 's enough if you 're
afraid of your own better feelings. *They 'll*
blackmail you. God, what a fool I was! Because I saw it coming years ago.

BILL. Saw what coming?

HUGO. Why, the crisis, the . . . the . . . well, *this*.
It was really so obvious that she was in love with
me. I pretended that I didn't know when my
father told me this evening. No, not pretended,
because officially I didn't know.

BILL. Officially?

HUGO.   Yes, like the communiqués during the war.
' Our forces are making a strategic retreat on a
front of 350 miles.' You know. Official truth.
And in the same way there 's an official part of the
mind that thinks and wishes the sort of things that
people ought to think and wish.   But there 's also
an unofficial part which doesn't believe in the communiqués, because it knows better—or anyhow it
knows differently.   Officially, Enid wasn't in love
with me, because it would have been such a damned
bore if she had been, but unofficially I knew she
was, and I was pleased and flattered.   Yes, and
what 's more, I did all I could to make her be more
in love with me.

BILL.   Even though you weren't in love with her
yourself ?

HUGO (*nods*).   I don't think you can know what a
luxury it is to have somebody in love with you.

BILL.   Why shouldn't I know ?

HUGO.   Things you have every day aren't luxuries.
You don't know what it is to be rather unattractive
physically.

BILL.   Nonsense.

HUGO.   No, no.   Unattractive, Bill, and shy, and
frightened.   You can't appreciate the luxury of
discovering that there 's at least *one* woman who
can be in love with you.   And the luxury of having
one woman you 're not more shy of because you 've
known her so long.   For you it 's so simple they
should fall in love with you.   Not for me.   That 's
why . . .

BILL.   That 's why you encouraged her to go on
loving you even though you weren't in love with
her yourself.   But, my good Hugo . . .

HUGO.   Yes, I know it was idiotic.

BILL. Loving some one who doesn't love you—
that's the worst thing, of course. But being
loved by somebody you can't love in return, in-
sistently and importunately loved—it's very nearly
as bad.

HUGO. I know. I know. It's awful.

BILL. Then why . . . ?

HUGO. But because the other person's love blackmails you? Yes, blackmails you. Like the beast-
liest little professional lounger in Hyde Park. ' If
you don't comply with what I demand,' that's what
it says to you, ' I'll go straight off and tell your
better self that you're a scoundrel; I'll go and
torture your defenceless conscience.' That's why
officially I never admitted that Enid was in love with
me. I didn't want to be blackmailed. But to-day
it all came out. There was no escape. I had to know
officially. And the blackmail began immediately.
' She loves you, she loves you. If you don't do
something about it, I'll go and stick pins into your
conscience.' Rather than run the risk of that I
proposed on the spot. But on the bloody spot.
(*He drinks*.)

BILL. Don't be a clown, Hugo. It's not funny.

HUGO (*in a changed tone*). You're quite right. It
wasn't. Do you know, Bill, I was terribly moved.
I really believed for a moment that everything was
coming right at last. I thought that if I tried hard
enough to love her I should really find myself
loving her—suddenly, like that—and be transfigured by loving; yes, and come alive. I thought
all that, and it was moving, moving. And then,
you know, at first she didn't want to say that she
loved me—just because she realised it would be
blackmailing me. Which touched me still more

—it was so honest. And I insisted, and at last I succeeded. God! How well I succeeded! It was awful, awful!

BILL. Why?

HUGO. Why, because it was then, when she began loving me, that I really knew I didn't love her—couldn't love her. . . . And the more loving she was the more coldly certain I became that I could never love her. Never, never. Oh, God, when I took her home just now! (*He shakes his head sharply, shaking off the memory, shuts his eyes against an importunate inward vision.*) How dreadful that was. But the blackmailing went on. More effectively than ever, just because it was so awful. Well, in a few months we shall be married. (*Laughing*) Good luck to us. (*He raises his glass and drinks.*) We'll go to Venice for the honeymoon, I think.

BILL (*rising from his chair*). No, you won't.

HUGO. Not to Venice? But all the best German honeymooners go to Venice.

BILL. Possibly, but you're coming with me to-morrow, Hugo. The ship leaves Tilbury at eleven. Come along. (*Takes him by the arm and drags him out of his seat.*) You've got some letters to write.

HUGO. But what are you talking about?

(BILL *leads him across the room to the writing-table, and makes him sit down before it.*)

BILL. One to your College, resigning your tutorship. One to your father. Here's a pen and some paper.

HUGO. But seriously, Bill . . .

BILL. I'm not going to allow you to destroy either yourself or that girl. (*Offers him the pen.*) Take it.

HUGO.   But I'm drunk, Bill.   Wait till to-morrow morning.   Let me think it over.

BILL.   No, no, at once.   You'd be sober in the morning.   You'd be reasonable.   Reasonable people never do anything.   Now begin.   I'll dictate.

HUGO.   But it's madness.

BILL.   I know.   That's just what it ought to be. Write now.   'My dear father——'

HUGO.   It's folly, it's criminal folly.

BILL.   Good.   'My dear father——'

HUGO (*writes*).   'My dear father——'   But I always write 'Dearest father——'

BILL.   Never mind.   He'll forgive you.   'My dear father, I have decided to accompany Bill Hamblin to-morrow. . . .'

HUGO.   But I haven't.

BILL.   You damned well have.

HUGO.   I won't be bullied.

BILL.   You will be bullied.   (*He takes him by the shoulders and shakes him.*)   Write, idiot, write!

HUGO.   For God's sake, Bill . . .

BILL.   Won't you be bullied?

HUGO.   Yes, yes, I'll be bullied.
      (BILL *stops shaking.*)
   I've *been* bullied.

BILL.   Good.   Let's see now, where were we? Ah yes!   'I have decided to accompany Bill Hamblin.'

HUGO (*writing*).   'I have decided to accompany Bill Hamblin.'

Curtain

ACT II

SCENE I

SCENE—*The same.* TIME—*Two months later.*

> (MRS. WENHAM *is sitting at her desk writing.*
> MR. WENHAM *enters, crosses the room and
> stands for a moment in nervous silence near
> her.* MRS. WENHAM *continues to write, then
> at last looks up.*)

MRS. WENHAM. Well, John ?

MR. WENHAM. I didn't want to interrupt you, my
dear.

MRS. WENHAM. You're not. What is it ?

MR. WENHAM. One was wondering, dear, whether
. . . whether you wouldn't care to . . . to join
us in the library.

MRS. WENHAM. Join whom ?

MR. WENHAM (*still more nervous*). Surely, my love,
I thought you knew. Young Mr. Capes is here.

MRS. WENHAM. Mr. Capes ?

MR. WENHAM. The young man through whom I've
been receiving these . . . these communications
from dear Hugo.

MRS. WENHAM. Oh, the medium. Yes, yes. I'd
forgotten his name. No, I don't think I'll come,
John.

MR. WENHAM. One would appreciate it so much if
you did.

MRS. WENHAM. I really have no time.

MR. WENHAM. Not more than half an hour, my
love.

MRS. WENHAM. Besides, John, I don't really much like that young man.

MR. WENHAM. No? One found him so . . . so charming oneself.

MRS. WENHAM. Too charming. That's the trouble. I don't like the butter laid on too thick.

MR. WENHAM. And gifted, wonderfully gifted. One simply can't doubt now that one's . . . well, in touch with poor Hugo.

MRS. WENHAM (*shrugs her shoulders*). All the same, John, I shall go on doubting until I hear definite news. After all, the only thing we know is that Hugo and Mr. Hamblin started out in their aeroplane to fly from Guiana to Cuba, and haven't been heard of since. But look at the map. There are hundreds of little islands where they could have come down. Besides, the machine had floats. It's only twelve days since they started. It seems to me still quite possible.

MR. WENHAM (*sighing and shaking his head*). One wishes one could think the same. There was really no hope. And now these communications through our young friend. . . . Well, they make it quite definite. The machine was forced down in a storm about thirty miles south of Haiti.

MRS. WENHAM. So he says. But why should one believe him?

MR. WENHAM. You'd know why, my love, if you'd only come and hear him. It's so obviously true —on the face of it. One can't doubt. That's why one was so anxious that you should . . .

MRS. WENHAM (*shaking her head*). I'd rather not.

MR. WENHAM. One had thought that perhaps . . . In this case . . . I mean, as it's dear Hugo——

M

MRS. WENHAM.   No, dear.   You know what I feel
about it.   Please don't insist.   (*Looking out of
the window.*)   And here's Enid coming across
the garden.   Go and open the door for her.   I
think it's still locked.

> (MR. WENHAM *goes and unlocks the French
> window.*)

Dressed in bright red to-day.   She really is extraordinary.

> (ENID *appears at the glass door and is let in by*
> MR. WENHAM.)

MR. WENHAM.   Good morning, my dear.

ENID (*her manner has a kind of defiant cheerfulness*).
Good morning.   Good morning, Alice.   (*Turning
back to* MR. WENHAM.)   Any news yet?

MR. WENHAM (*shakes his head*).   Not what *you*
would call news, dear Enid.   But so far as oneself
is concerned . . .

ENID.   What do you mean?

MRS. WENHAM.   John means that he's had a message through the medium.   It's supposed to be
from Hugo.

ENID (*laughing with sudden violence—a laugh that is
intended to be deliberately contemptuous, but rings
a little hysterically, on the verge of going out of
control*).   Oh, if that's all.

MR. WENHAM (*gravely*).   It's a very great deal,
Enid dear.   In fact, I'm afraid it's all we have
now, all that's left.   (*To* MRS. WENHAM)   I shall
be in the library if you want me, my love.

> (MR. WENHAM *goes out.   There is a silence.*)

MRS. WENHAM.   I don't want to be critical and inter-
fering, Enid;   but I really do think it's rather a
mistake to wear that red dress.

ENID.   Why?

MRS. WENHAM.   Well, surely the colour 's a little inappropriate in the circumstances.

ENID.   You 'd like me to wear black, would you ?

MRS. WENHAM.   No, no.   Only something rather quieter.   It may be a foolishness on my part ; but it seems to me that in this dreadful uncertainty . . .

ENID.   But I 'm certain, Alice, absolutely certain. He isn't dead.   (*She clasps her hands violently together.*)   I know he isn't.   He can't be.   I won't let him be dead.

MRS. WENHAM.   I only hope you 're right.

ENID (*with sudden anger*).   Why don't you say you *know* I 'm right ?   Why do you doubt ?   You 're killing him with all this doubt of yours.   And his father 's even worse.   Deliberately killing him with denial.   Yes, denial.   He doesn't *want* Hugo to be alive.   He 'd like him to be dead, so that he can talk to him through these beastly mediums.

MRS. WENHAM.   But, Enid, you 're mad !

ENID (*beginning to break down uncontrollably*).   You all want him to be dead.

MRS. WENHAM.   You mustn't say such things.

ENID (*sobbing*).   You want him to be dead, you want him to be dead.

> (MRS. WENHAM *gets up and goes over to where* ENID *is sitting and stands by her with a hand on her shoulder.*)
>
> (*Jerking herself away from under the touching hand*) No, don't.

MRS. WENHAM.   My dear, my dear.

> (ENID *suffers herself to be touched.   There is a silence, broken only by the sound of* ENID'S *sobbing.*)

You know, I really think there 's a good chance of Hugo's being all right.

(ENID *shakes her head.*)

I was saying so to John only a moment ago. One's only got to look at the map. All those hundreds of islands . . .

ENID. No, no. It's no good. I know he's dead, really. That's why I got so angry just now. I'm sorry. But if you knew how awful it was, Alice. (*She starts crying again.*)

MRS. WENHAM. Poor Enid. (*She pats her shoulder.*) Be brave. You must be brave.

ENID. I cared for him, so much, Alice. (*She puts her hand to her side.*) It's so awful, the pain. Like a kind of hole, where one's heart ought to be. Ever since he went away. Why did he go away, like that ? Why, why ?

MRS. WENHAM (*sighs and shakes her head*). Some mad idea. It was that wild young Hamblin, I suppose.

ENID (*after a pause. She is sitting bent forward, her elbows on her knees, her face between her hands.*) That morning when I came to tell you we were engaged and heard he was gone—that was when it began, this emptiness, I mean, this horrible, aching, anxious hole. Because I knew even then he'd gone for ever.

MRS. WENHAM. But, dear, you mustn't say that. There really *is* a chance. You're doing what you were reproaching us for doing a moment ago.

ENID. Gone for ever from *me*—that's what I meant. Because he didn't really love me, you know. He only wanted to love me, and perhaps he suddenly realised that he couldn't, simply couldn't. And that's why he went. I oughtn't to have said yes when he asked me. It was wrong, it was stupid ; I ought to have realised.

MRS. WENHAM. But no, darling, we all know how deeply attached he was to you.

ENID (*nodding slowly*). You can be deeply attached and at the same time have a kind of hatred of the person you 're attached to.

MRS. WENHAM. What nonsense !

ENID. A kind of fatal, uncontrollable, physical hatred. Perhaps that was why Hugo . . . No, it 's dreadful, it 's dreadful.

MRS. WENHAM. You mustn't think that sort of thing, Enid. It 's stupid, it 's morbid.

ENID. All the same, I do think it—constantly. I wonder and wonder. And the more I wonder, the worse it seems. (*Pause.*) No, I oughtn't to have said yes. It was madness. But I did care so much. Oh, Alice, I cared so terribly much.

MRS. WENHAM. And he cared too. It 's absurd to say he didn't. And now I simply forbid you to go on thinking these horrible morbid thoughts any more.

ENID (*making an impatient gesture*). Oh, don't use that tiresome, stupid word, Alice.

MRS. WENHAM. What word ? Morbid ? But they *are* morbid ; I 'm sorry.

ENID. What you mean is that they 're just thoughts you don't understand, thoughts you don't happen to have had yourself.

MRS. WENHAM. Thank goodness ! I 've no desire to have morbid thoughts. And I think that you ought to make an effort to keep your mind off them. It 's almost all a question of will.

ENID (*uttering an ironic little laugh*). All right, I 'll make an effort. (*She leans back in her chair and holds out her arms, clenching her fists as she does so.*) I 'll will not to think about any truth that

MR. WENHAM (*nodding*). Yes, Haiti. Our young friend here (*he indicates* CAPES) was quite right.

ENID (*with a sudden burst of angry, hysterical laughter*). You're so pleased that he should be right. Much more pleased than you would be if the telegram had said that poor Hugo was safe and well. Yes, *much* more pleased.

MRS. WENHAM. Enid! How can you?

ENID. But it's true. (*She checks herself with an effort and is silent for a moment, biting her handkerchief; then in another voice*) I'm sorry, Mr. Wenham. I think I'd better go. Forgive me.

MR. WENHAM. There's nothing to forgive, my dear. One knows what you must be feeling. And there are no consolations, Enid dear, except the faith, the knowledge . . . well, that after all dear Hugo isn't dead . . . that his spirit is with us . . . still.

HUBERT (*in a rather unctuous, musical voice that harmonises well with a darkly handsome, slightly clerical appearance*). Yes, his spirit is still with us.

ENID (*who has come to rest with her elbows on the mantelpiece, her face hidden*). Only his spirit. (*A pause; then breaking out*) But I don't want his spirit. I want Hugo, I want Hugo!

Curtain

SCENE II

SCENE—*The same.* TIME—*Ten months later.*

> (*Except for a few streaks of phosphorescent paint on various objects, the stage, when the curtain rises, is in darkness. The voices are heard, but the speakers are not seen.*)

MR. WENHAM. What do you think, Enid? Is it safe to turn on the light now?

ENID. Perhaps we'd better wait a moment longer. You know what a shock it is to him, when he's woken too quickly out of his trance.

MR. WENHAM. Oh, of course, one wouldn't dream of . . . of taking any risk at our young friend's expense. But it seems to me it must be the best part of five minutes since the last manifestation.

ENID. Do you think so? Time's apt to seem very long when one's sitting in the dark like this. Besides, he's always more tired when the séance has been a very successful one. So perhaps we ought to give him a little longer than usual.

MR. WENHAM. You're quite right, my dear. I wouldn't worry if it wasn't that Alice was expecting me to come up and say good-night to the children.

ENID (*impatiently*). After all, she can wait another minute or two.

MR. WENHAM. Yes, but one doesn't like to keep the little ones awake beyond the appointed hour.

ENID. Well, even they won't die of it.

MR. WENHAM. No, no, of course not. But all the same . . .

ENID. Wasn't he simply wonderful this evening ?
I don't think we 've ever had such extraordinary
physical manifestations as to-day.

MR. WENHAM. Yes, they were certainly very remarkable.

ENID. I 've never known the table move so violently
as it did this time.   And then when the concertina
started playing inside the cage—that was too
extraordinary.

MR. WENHAM. And the phosphorescent paint made
it quite easy to see.   I was able to watch its move-
ments very closely.   Did you notice that it didn't
just go in and out, but seemed to . . . well, to
writhe from side to side as well ?

ENID. Yes, I noticed that.

MR. WENHAM. Rather like a snake, if you were to
hang it up by the tail.   Very curious.   I seemed
to recognise the tune, by the way.   Wasn't it
something classical ?

ENID. Yes, it was a bit of that air out of *Figaro*—
you know, the duet of the letter.   Hugo had a
special liking for it, don't you remember ?   He
was constantly whistling it.

MR. WENHAM. Of course.   That was why one
found it so familiar.   I 'd forgotten it completely.
Strange that one should be reminded in this way.
Very strange.

ENID. Very wonderful, I think.   (*A little pause.*)

MR. WENHAM (*in a changed tone, preoccupied*).
What about turning on the light now, Enid ?
It couldn't do any harm, and one really must be
trotting up to the children.

ENID (*with a touch of contempt*).   Oh, very well, then.
Sit where you are.   I 'll do it.

(ENID *is heard fumbling in the darkness, then*

the room is suddenly flooded with light.
HUBERT CAPES *is seen lying back limply
in a chair in the corner. The mediumistic
apparatus is scattered round him, trumpets,
tambourines, etc., and in a large parrot-cage,
hanging vertically, a concertina.*)

MR. WENHAM (*blinking and holding his hands over
his eyes*).   It certainly does seem very bright all
of a sudden.

ENID (*who has crossed the room and is bending over
HUBERT*).   Hubert !   (*She touches his shoulder,
then his face.*)   Hubert !   (*To* WENHAM) It must
have been a very deep trance.

MR. WENHAM (*rising*).   Perhaps if one were to blow
on his eyelids . . .

ENID.   No, don't.   He's beginning to wake up.
Hubert !

(HUBERT *utters a deep sigh ; his eyes begin to
flutter open.*)

Wake up, Hubert, wake up !

HUBERT (*faintly*).   Where am I ?   Oh, it's you.
(*He takes her hand.*)   I feel as though I've come
back from a very long way this time.   Enormously far.   I feel sort of (*makes a vague gesture*)—
I don't know what.   Sort of not there.   As
though I've come to bits.

ENID.   Poor Hubert !   You were wonderful to-
night.   That's why you're so tired.

HUBERT.   Did the spirits manifest well ?

MR. WENHAM.   Quite remarkably.   There was a
moment when the concertina began to play . . .
but we'll discuss that later, if you don't mind.
(*He looks at his watch.*)   The children are expecting one to come and say good-night.   Oh dear, oh
dear, I'm ten minutes late already.   Enid dear,

see that our young friend has everything he wants. Forgive me. (*He hurries out of the room.*)

ENID. He's like a schoolboy. Too ridiculous, a man being frightened of his wife like that.

(HUBERT *sighs deeply and shuts his eyes again.*) Poor Hubert! (*Her voice is tenderly solicitous, she lays her hand on his forehead.*) Are you terribly tired?

(HUBERT *nods without speaking.*) Would you like me to get you a glass of wine, or some Bovril, or something?

(HUBERT *shakes his head.*) You're sure you don't want anything? (ENID *sits down on the arm of his chair.*)

HUBERT. No, just keep your hand on my forehead, that's all. It's so soothing. I feel as though there were a kind of current of strength and serenity passing out from you. A river of healing. I shall be quite fresh and strong again in a few minutes. I think if some one were ill, you could cure him, just by touching him.

ENID. Do you think so?

HUBERT. I know it. I can feel it in myself.

ENID. Well, I'm glad. Because it means that I can make you some little return for what you did for me.

HUBERT. But I've done nothing.

ENID. Nothing, perhaps, so far as any one else is concerned. But you saved my life, Hubert. In those terrible days just after the news of poor Hugo's death, I wanted to die, I thought I was going to die; but I didn't. I suppose one doesn't die of unhappiness like that. One's tougher than one thinks. So I made up my mind to kill myself. Yes, and I should have killed myself if it hadn't been for you.   You made me realise that he was not really dead, but still near, still interested and wanting me to go on living.   Oh, I shall never forget that first message that you brought me ! You saved me, Hubert.

HUBERT.   Or rather, it was the truth that saved you —the truth expressing itself through me.

ENID.   Yes, but you helped the truth, Hubert.   You were so sweet to me, so divinely kind and good.

HUBERT (*making a gesture of deprecation*).   No, no.

ENID.   Yes, divinely.   You were like some one sent from heaven to save me.

HUBERT.   You mustn't talk so extravagantly. Though in one sense, of course, there 's a certain truth in what you say.   Because I 'm a sort of instrument.   Chosen for some inscrutable reason —in spite of unworthiness.   Chosen to make known the truth.   Chosen to help you and all who have an unhappiness like yours.   Poor Enid !   It made my heart bleed to see you so hopelessly and inconsolably miserable !

ENID.   He seemed so utterly dead and gone.   And yet I ought to have had faith.   I believe in the resurrection of the body and the life everlasting. Haven't I been repeating that Sunday after Sunday, all my life ?   But when it came to the point I couldn't help feeling that death was the end of everything, just a black, ghastly pit.

HUBERT.   What a terrible thing to believe !

ENID.   You taught me more than all the books and creeds and churches ever taught me.   I thought I believed ; but I suppose I didn't really.

HUBERT.   It 's the difference between seeing in a glass darkly and seeing face to face.   That 's the wonderful thing about spiritualism : it can show

ENID. Of course you don't ! In *that* tone.

HUBERT. I 'm sorry, I was on edge. But it was partly your fault. One doesn't like to be doubted and questioned, and cross-examined. Enid !

(HUBERT *holds out his arms to her, but* ENID *shakes her head and turns away. He lets his arms fall again rather sheepishly. There is a silence.*)

ENID (*almost meditatively*). And yet you used to care for me. At least I thought you did.

HUBERT. But, darling, I still do. What is this absurd, stupid idea you 've got into your head ?

ENID. It was you who put it there . . . by being so sweet to me when I was unhappy, so gentle and tenderly loving. Yes, you put it into my head by giving me something to compare the present with . . .

HUBERT. But the present 's the same as the past. It 's not as though we 'd quarrelled or had a scene, or . . .

ENID. That 's just what makes it so awful. I wish we had quarrelled. A quarrel would have been something definite, something to put one's finger on. But you 've just noiselessly faded away from me. Faded away out of love, out of my life, like a ghost, like (*suddenly laughing hysterically*) . . . like the Cheshire cat.

HUBERT. But, Enid, it 's not true.

ENID. Then why is it you make me feel that everything 's changed ?

HUBERT (*plaintively rational*). I really can't think. I suppose something must have changed in you.

ENID (*sarcastically laughing*). I like that ; that 's very good. But do you think a woman doesn't *feel* when a man has stopped loving her ? Do you edition to look forward to. Another twenty thousand at four-and-six—or why not six shillings while we 're about it ?   It 's a delightful prospect. (*He helps himself to a sandwich.*)

MRS. WENHAM.   It certainly seems a great number, considering the subject of the book.

MR. GRAY.   Oh, the subject 's all right.   Believe an old publisher, Mrs. Wenham.   Spiritualism 's one of the soundest of all non-fiction subjects.   Almost as good as theology.   Much sounder than politics, for example.   Why, I 'd far rather publish Mrs. Piper than Winston Churchill.   No, it 's the price I 'm thinking of.   It 's considering the price that the sale 's so remarkable.

MR. WENHAM (*uncomfortably—he does not like these commercial discussions*).   One always did consider the price rather excessive.

MR. GRAY.   I know you did.   But admit, you were wrong.   We asked a guinea, and sixteen thousand people have given it.   *Vox populi, vox Dei.*   Mrs. Wenham, I consider that it 's a testimonial to the value of your husband's message.   The truth about the Great Beyond—why, it 's *worth* a guinea.   People wouldn't pay a guinea for Edgar Wallace.   To my mind, that 's very significant. (*He helps himself to another sandwich.*)

MRS. WENHAM.   Quite so.   I see what you mean.

MR. GRAY (*his mouth full of sandwich*).   And I don't mind admitting it, Mrs. Wenham ; it was the popular response to your husband's book that finally converted me to spiritualism.   Something that sixteen thousand men and women are prepared to pay a guinea for—and, mind you, there 's nothing that people are so avaricious about as books—well, I said to myself, there must be something in it. Besides, when a man like your husband—an expert accountant, mark you!—affirms his belief in spiritualism, well, it's probable, to say the least of it, that spirits exist. It's practically certain, in fact. (*He takes a chocolate éclair.*) I think you'll agree with me, Mr. Wenham.

MR. WENHAM. Well, of course, one's ready to give more credit to a . . . well, a trained intelligence . . .

MR. GRAY. A trained intelligence; that's it exactly.

MR. WENHAM. But it's not simply a question of authority, of course. It's the facts that matter. The only merit one claims for one's book is that it's a collection of facts.

MR. GRAY. A positive mine.

MR. WENHAM. All one has done is to bring together the evidence. Dispassionately, as far as that's possible, with intelligence. . . .

MR. GRAY. The trained intelligence of the expert accountant. Don't forget that.

MR. WENHAM. But, of course, it's thanks to the powers of our young friend, Hubert Capes, that there's any evidence to collect. I consider him one of the most . . . the most richly talented of living mediums.

MR. GRAY. You don't say so.

MRS. WENHAM. Some more tea, Mr. Gray?

MR. GRAY. With pleasure. (*He passes his cup.*)

MRS. WENHAM. Cut Mr. Gray a slice of cake, John.

MR. WENHAM (*cutting*). You see, he's gifted in such a variety of ways. As a producer of physical manifestations, he's second to none. D. D. Home himself never excelled him. And at the same time he has an extraordinary receptivity for purely mental and spiritual communications. (*He hands the cake on the end of the knife to* MR. GRAY.)

For book tests and cross-correspondence tests he 's
. . . well, unique.   To one's own mind, some of the
ones recorded in the book are even more . . . more
convincing than Mrs. Verrall's and Mrs. Piper's.

MRS. WENHAM.   Pass me your cup, John.

MR GRAY (*with a sigh, profoundly*).   Well, well,
there are more things in heaven and earth, Hor-
atio, than are dreamt of in *your* philosophy. . . .
(*There is a silence.   He eats his cake meditatively.
Turning to* MRS. WENHAM) I suppose you share
your husband's interests in this absorbing subject,
Mrs. Wenham.

MRS. WENHAM (*coldly*).   To some extent.   But when
one has a house to look after, and a couple of wild
little boys, there isn't much time for spiritualism.

MR. GRAY.   Quite, quite.   A woman's work is never
done, as the poet says.

MR. WENHAM (*changing the subject, with an arti-
ficial offhandedness*).   It 's a pity Miss Deckle had
to run off like that ; I 'd have liked you to have a
talk with her.   A most interesting girl.   She 's
been my . . . well, shall I be Irish and say she 's
been my right-hand man ?   The book would
never have got written without her.   She ought in
justice to have her name on the title-page along
with one's own.   But she didn't want to.

MR. GRAY.   A labour of love, in fact.

MR. WENHAM.   In a very literal sense, even.   She
and my Hugo were actually . . . well, betrothed.

MR. GRAY.   Poor girl, poor girl !

MR. WENHAM (*sighing*).   She suffered very griev-
ously, when Hugo passed on.   A very highly
strung, emotional nature, you know.

MR. GRAY.   They 're apt to be, these young people,
I find.   Rather morbid, even.

MR. WENHAM. It was a terrible blow, of course. But in the end suffering always purifies and uplifts.

MRS. WENHAM. Does it always? I sometimes wonder. (*She gets up.*) But I must go and see that my children aren't misbehaving. (*She moves towards the door.*)

MR. GRAY. Allow me. (*He hurries across the room to open for her.*)

MRS. WENHAM. Thank you. I'll see you later, Mr. Gray. (*She goes out.*)

MR. GRAY (*pulling out his case*). What do you say to a small cigar, Mr. Wenham?

MR. WENHAM. Thanks. One never smokes.

MR. GRAY (*selecting a cigar and lighting it*). Wise man. I wish I didn't (*leaning back in his chair and blowing a cloud of smoke into the air*). Well, well, it's all a very sad and touching story. That gallant youth lost there in the tropic seas. And this poor girl, waiting here. For men must work and women must weep. (*He shakes his head.*) Sad, very sad. Still, all's well that ends well. And I think we can say that this *has* ended pretty well, all things considered. Contact established with the dead . . . or rather (*he waves his cigar*) the happily living. Grief consoled. Tears, idle tears, completely dried. And finally, this extraordinary, this truly magnificent sale for your book. Sixteen thousand! I shall be sending you another little cheque quite soon, you know. And not such a very little one either, my boy. (*He winks and shakes a fat forefinger at* MR. WENHAM.) Twelve hundred pounds. Not bad, eh? It'll bring your royalties up to well over three thousand. Oh, I assure you, there are precious few of my authors who can make that with a single book—to say nothing of a first book, mark you. Why, if it weren't absolutely necessary that an author should begin writing some time, no publisher would ever look at a first book. Too risky, too unprofitable. And now you come along and prove the rule with a glorious exception. Sixteen thousand copies!

MR. WENHAM (*who has been listening with signs of embarrassment*). Of course, one's very pleased that so many people should . . . should be interested in the truth. (*He gets up and rings the bell*).

MR. GRAY. *Magna est veritas et praevalebit*, as we used to say at school. But at the same time, don't forget that the labourer is worthy of his hire. I'm so glad now that I was firm about the book being priced at a guinea. At twelve-and-six, sales would have been hardly any larger. We should just have lost forty per cent. of our profits. To no purpose. *Cui bono*, in a word.

MR. WENHAM. You may be right.

MR. GRAY. I know I'm right.

(*Enter the* MAID.)

MR. WENHAM (*to the* MAID). Will you clear away the tea things? (*To* GRAY) We might go into the library meanwhile.

MR. GRAY (*rising*). I'm at your disposition.

MR. WENHAM. I have some interesting early works on accountancy I'd like to show you.

(*They go out. The* MAID *is left. She hums to herself as she clears the table. She goes out with the cake-stand, returns, goes out again with the tray. During her second absence enter* HUBERT *and* ENID.)

ENID (*very much agitated*). It's really intolerable the way they chase one from room to room.

HUBERT. But mayn't Mr. Wenham go into his own library if he wants to ? (*Goes over to the tea-table and looks round.*) Damn. I'd hoped there might be something left.

ENID (*who has not heard these last words*). He did it on purpose. He knew we were there.

HUBERT. What nonsense ! (*His annoyance at not finding anything to eat has strengthened him against her. His tone is sharp.*) You saw how surprised and embarrassed he was.

ENID. *He* knew all right.

(*The* MAID *re-enters, silently.*)

I expect it was that cat Alice who sent him to . . .

HUBERT. Sh ! Sh ! (*Loudly*) The book seems to be doing very well. Gray was saying something about sixteen thousand copies when you interrupted him.

ENID. Isn't it simply disgusting, the way he says ' Sixteen thousand,' as though it were a mixture between something holy and something good to eat. Ugh !

HUBERT (*in a low voice, after glancing at the* MAID). I think perhaps it might be better . . .

ENID (*with contemptuous impatience*). All right, all right. (*Loudly*) Wasn't it nice and warm to-day ? Or was it nice and cold ? I forget which. (*She gets up, much agitated, and begins to walk about the room. A brief silence.*)

HUBERT. Decidedly warm. The thermometer was at seventy-two this morning.

(*Another silence. The* MAID, *who has been folding the cloth and putting away the tea-table, goes out.*)

ENID. At last ! She was doing it on purpose, you know.

HUBERT. Doing what ? (*His tone is snappy and resentful.*)

ENID. Being so slow. Just to spite us.

HUBERT. What a ridiculous exaggeration !

ENID. Exaggeration, exaggeration ! Now you 're beginning to talk like Alice.

HUBERT. Alice is quite right. (*He turns on her.*) And look here, Enid, I absolutely refuse to be made a fool of any more in this way.

ENID. What way ?

HUBERT (*trembling with rage*). Being dragged out of rooms the moment any one comes in ; and having my conversations interrupted ; and being pulled here and pushed there ; and having you answer for me and saying I don't want any tea—when I do.

ENID (*her anger fallen, in a sudden access of penitence*). But, my darling, I had no idea. Why didn't you say you were hungry ? I 'll ring and ask Mary to bring you something.

HUBERT (*checking her as she moves towards the bell*). Certainly not.

ENID. But if you want it.

HUBERT. It 's too late now.

ENID. Not a bit.

HUBERT. Besides, I 've lost my appetite. (*He turns away, a dignified martyr.*)

ENID. Oh, I 'm so wretched.

HUBERT. A little late in the day.

ENID. It 's this devil that possesses me. Making me do things that are stupid and harmful and against myself, against you. (*Appealingly*) Hubert !

HUBERT (*still averted*). And if you imagine that this sort of thing creates the right atmosphere for getting into touch with any one on the other side, you 're very much mistaken.

ENID. Forgive me, Hubert.

HUBERT. What I need is soothing and sympathy and understanding. Instead of which I 'm harried and shouted at as though I were a kind of criminal. I 'm sure the séance this evening won't be a success. How can it be, with my nerves in this state? I 've a good mind to tell Mr. Wenham that I can't do anything this evening.

ENID. Well, there 's no reason why you should.

HUBERT. There *is* a reason. He 's arranged specially for Gray to come.

ENID. That awful Gray? *He* doesn't matter. Let me go and tell Mr. Wenham that you can't manage a séance to-day.

HUBERT. No, no.

ENID (*rising*). You can rest here quietly, while I go.

HUBERT. No, I won't have it. Sit down. What would he think? He 'd see there was something wrong. You 'd have to explain. *I 'd* have to explain. It would be very awkward. (*Resignedly heroic*) No, I 'll go through with it somehow.

ENID (*takes his hand and strokes it. Almost whispering*). Forgive me, Hubert, forgive me. (*There is a long silence.*)

    (*Enter* MR. WENHAM *and* MR. GRAY. *The others spring up and apart rather guiltily.*)

MR. WENHAM. One was wondering, Hubert, if you were ready to begin.

HUBERT (*breezily, with a smile*). Oh, whenever you like.

ENID (*anxiously*). You 're sure you 're feeling up to it? Hubert?

HUBERT (*annoyed*). Of course I am. (*To* MR. WENHAM) Shall we start at once?

MR. WENHAM. Well, why not ? Turn on the light, Enid. I 'm going to draw the curtains. (*He goes to the window.*)

HUBERT. Is this your first experience of this kind of thing, Mr. Gray ?

MR. GRAY. Positively the first. To tell you the truth, I 've not given the subject my serious consideration before reading our friend's book. I 'd even been sceptical—the scepticism of ignorance. The book enlightened and convinced me ! Truth is stranger than fiction. As an old publisher, I ought to have known it, of course. (*He shakes his head.*) Most extraordinary, most extraordinary.

HUBERT. Only because you 're not used to it. If you lived as I do, on the borderland, so to speak, between the two worlds, you wouldn't find the other side any more extraordinary than this. Less, really. Because the other side is a moral world, and this isn't. What happens there is what ought to happen. So it seems more normal really than this world, where the things that ought to happen so seldom do happen.

MR. GRAY. Quite, quite. A most illuminating thought. (*To* ENID) What 's that, may I ask, Miss Deckle ?

ENID (*who is carrying a large box which she has taken out of a cupboard*). The musical-box. (*She puts it down on a small table.*)

MR. GRAY. A musical-box ? What for ?

ENID (*curtly—she cannot bear talking to him*). To make music.

HUBERT (*making up with a specially unctuous politeness for* ENID'S *bad manners*). It 's kept going all through the séance. An atmosphere of harmonious sound. It helps me to get through.

MR. WENHAM (*who has finished with the curtains*).
Music helps the medium to . . . well, I was going
to say concentrate ; but that 's the wrong word ;
because you can't go into a trance without doing
the exact opposite to concentrating. You 've got
to *ex*centrate, if you see what I mean—think of
nothing. Music seems to help one to do that.
(*To* HUBERT) You 'll sit in your usual place, I
suppose ?

HUBERT. Yes.

MR. WENHAM. Put the trumpets and the accordion
on the bookshelf, will you, Enid ?

ENID. I 'm just getting everything ready.
(ENID *goes back and forth to the cupboard,
collecting various objects, such as tambourines,
cardboard trumpets, a concertina, sheets of
cardboard covered with luminous paint, etc.*)

MR. WENHAM (*to* MR. GRAY). We 're just preparing
for the simplest physical manifestations. For
some one who 's new to spiritualism, like yourself,
they 're . . . well, the most startling phenomena.

MR. GRAY. Quite.

MR. WENHAM. Though not, of course . . . the
most significant as evidence of survival. Should
we begin, Hubert ?

HUBERT. Certainly, Mr. Wenham. (*He goes to his
seat in the corner.*)
(*The others take chairs across the angle in front
of him.* ENID *sits by the little table on which
the musical-box stands.*)

ENID. I 'll see to the music. (*She gives the handle a
couple of turns ; a few bars of a hymn tinkle out.*)
That's working all right. Shall I turn off the light?

HUBERT (*who is lying back in his chair, relaxed, with
closed eyes*). Yes, I 'm ready.

(ENID *goes to the door and turns the switch.
The room is plunged in darkness. Patches
of phosphorescent paint gleam here and
there.*)

MR. WENHAM. Can you find your way back, Enid ?

ENID. Yes, thanks. Here I am. (*The music starts
playing and tinkles on without interruption, the
same hymn-tune, again and again.*)

MR. WENHAM. He's going off into a trance now.
It generally takes a minute or two.

MR. GRAY. Oughtn't one to be silent, in that case ?

MR. WENHAM. No, he prefers one to go on talking.
Sometimes it even helps if one sings. Something
simple that every one knows. A hymn, for
example. 'Abide with me' always seems to be
particularly . . . well . . . effective . . .

MR. GRAY. How can you tell when he's gone off
into the trance ?

MR. WENHAM. By the way he breathes. A certain
. . . a certain stertorousness. And then, almost at
once, you hear the voice of the control.

MR. GRAY. The who ?

MR. WENHAM. The control, the spirit guide. Every
medium has a control on the other side. It's the
control that . . . well, introduces the other spirits.
In our young friend's case, the principal control is
a certain Dr. Ledoux.

MR. GRAY. Yes. I remember your book. A
Frenchman.

MR. WENHAM. Of French extraction. But he
appears to have practised in London while he was
. . . while he was . . . well, in a word, alive.
An interesting personality. Rather eccentric.
(*To* ENID) You're not getting tired turning that
handle, are you, Enid ?

ENID. No, thanks.
> (*A silence. The hymn-tune tinkles out steadily, again and again.*)

MR. GRAY. It's a curious sensation, sitting here in the dark.   One has a sort of expectant feeling that almost anything might happen. (*With a little laugh*) And in point of fact, it *does* happen.

MR. WENHAM. Well, not *anything*. You mustn't imagine that the spirit world is . . . well, fantastic or irregular.   It has its natural laws, like the material world.   Little by little we're beginning to formulate them.
> (*Silence. Curious sounds begin to come from the medium. The music stops.*)

Ah, do you hear ? He seems to be going off.

MR. GRAY. Is he unconscious during the trance ?

MR. WENHAM. The surface of his mind's asleep. But of course the deeper layers are unusually active.

HUBERT (*muttering in a voice quite unlike his normal voice, guttural, deep, with a foreign accent*). Good eve . . . good . . . goo . . . goo . . . (*stammering*) good eve . . .

MR. WENHAM. That's the control beginning to come through. (*In a loud and cheerful tone, rather like that which one uses to address a member of the lower classes*) Good evening, Dr. Ledoux.   It's nice to hear your voice again.

HUBERT. Good evening.

MR. WENHAM. And how are you ? How are all our friends on the other side ?

HUBERT. *Très bien, très bien, merci.* But there is a new face here to-night.

MR. WENHAM. Just a friend, Dr. Ledoux ; an interested friend who wanted to see the manifestations.

MR. GRAY.   In all reverence, mind you ; not mere idle curiosity.

HUBERT.   H'm, I do not much like him.

MR. WENHAM.   Oh, come, Dr. Ledoux ! (*To* MR. GRAY) I told you he was a most eccentric personality. (*To the medium*) Mr. Gray is deeply interested.

HUBERT.   He is not grey, he is black.   Enid !   Why do you not speak to me this evening ?

ENID.   I was waiting till Mr. Wenham had finished. How is Hugo ?

HUBERT.   Hugo is *très bien, merci.*

ENID.   Can you get him to come ?

HUBERT.   Yes, I think he will come. *Viens donc, viens. Mais, mais, mais, mais, qu'est-ce qu'il fait, ce garçon-la ?   Mais, mais, mais, mais . . .* (*The voice tails off into an incoherent mumble.*)

MR. GRAY.   What 's happened to him now ?

MR. WENHAM.   Oh, he 's just gone back again for a moment.   You mustn't mind if he 's rude to you, by the way.   Dr. Ledoux is often very rude.   It 's a certain perverted sense of humour in him.   There 's something . . . well, rather impish about him.

HUBERT.   *Il va venir bientôt.* Not at present, though.   He is thinking much of you, Mr. Wenham, much of Enid, too.   More than usual. (*Calling sharply*) Black !

MR. GRAY.   Does he mean me, do you think ?

HUBERT.   Yes, of course, I mean you.   Why do you not ask me that question about your father ?

MR. GRAY.   Most extraordinary.   I was just thinking of asking him if he knew my father's name. *Do* you happen to know it, Dr. Ledoux ?

HUBERT.   *Il s'appelle Alfred.   Je le connais.* He asks if you still have *sa chaîne de montre en or et platine*?

MR. WENHAM.   You mean the one that Hugo was
    so fond of ?

ENID.   Yes, the one that Hugo was always . . .
    (*The door suddenly flies open, the figures of*
    HUGO *and* BILL *are seen silhouetted against
    the light outside.*)

HUGO.   What on earth's happening here ? (*He
    turns on the light.*)
    (*The concertina falls with a crash to the
    ground.* HUBERT, *who is lying back limply
    in his chair, utters a cry of pain, covers his eyes
    with his hand, then slips sideways in a faint.
    The others spring up.*)

HUGO.   Oh, a séance.   I'm so sorry.   Have I spoilt
    the best effect ?
    (*He advances into the room.*)
    Well, father.   Like the proverbial bad penny . . .
    (MR. WENHAM *stands petrified.*   ENID *steps
    forward.*)

ENID.   Hugo !

HUGO.   Why, Enid !   I didn't know *you'd* taken to
    ghosts.

BILL (*in black spectacles, groping his way blindly
    after* HUGO).   Hugo !   Why the devil do you
    leave me alone here in the dark ? (*He stumbles
    against a chair.*)   Damnation !   Where are you ?
    (ENID *stretches out her arm ; he comes up
    against it.*)
    Why . . .?

HUGO (*meanwhile stepping back and taking him by
    the arm*).   Here I am, Bill. (*Patting his arm.
    To* ENID) He can't see.

ENID.   It's all right.   Take my hand.

Curtain

ACT III

(Mrs. Wenham, Hugo *and* Bill, *standing near the French window by which* Bill *and* Hugo *have just entered.*)

Mrs. Wenham. But why, Hugo? Tell me why you never told us.

Bill (*who has been groping about with his hands, peevishly*). Can't you give me a chair, Hugo? For God's sake give me a chair.

Hugo. Sorry, Bill. (*Pushes up a chair.*)
    (Bill *sits down.*)
There you are ; make yourself comfortable.

Bill. None of your horrible bedside manner, now. I won't have you patronising me.

Hugo. Sorry, I didn't mean to be bedside-ish.

Bill. That only makes it worse. It means you can't help being insulting.

Mrs. Wenham. But why, Hugo, tell me why?

Hugo. Why? Well, I don't know. Why did we go on letting people think we were dead, Bill?

Bill. Why not? Mayn't one play a practical joke if one wants to?

Hugo. Well . . . of course it sounds idiotic . . . but in a certain sense it *was* all a kind of joke. It seemed so amusing at the time. Bill and I—well, I don't exactly know how to describe it—we were kind of drunk with adventure. Weren't we, Bill?

Bill. Were we? (*Shrugs his shoulders.*) Anyhow, it's the morning after now.

Hugo. And then, of course, when one had carried

on the joke for a certain time, it was difficult to go back. One was a bit ashamed. So one felt one had to stick to it. If it hadn't been for Bill's accident, I suppose we'd still be playing our joke.

MRS. WENHAM. But what a horrible, wicked, cruel joke, Hugo!

HUGO. But how could I have foreseen that this would happen?

BILL (*laughing with sudden savagery*). The fun's really only just beginning.

MRS. WENHAM (*indignantly*). Mr. Hamblin!

(HUGO *makes an imploring gesture, begging her to be silent. She checks herself and turns to* HUGO.)

But even if your father hadn't written this book, Hugo—even then, it would have been a hateful, cruel thing to do.

HUGO. Oh, I know, I know. But there were also serious reasons, Alice. One's simply got to be cruel sometimes. There's a kind of ultimate selfishness that's sacred and imperative; I simply had to escape—go right away, be somebody else. It seemed a heaven-sent opportunity.

MRS. WENHAM. A heaven-sent opportunity to make your poor father suffer.

BILL. One for you, Mrs. Wenham!

MRS. WENHAM. I can't think how you did it, Hugo —you who used to be so considerate.

HUGO. Well, I suppose it was one of the things I learnt out there, Alice—*not* to be too considerate.

BILL. One for you, Hugo!

HUGO. And I can tell you, it was a difficult lesson. Learning to be hard, when one's naturally soft; learning to be clear and definite when one's native weather is fog—oh, it wasn't easy.

MRS. WENHAM. Now, Hugo, you can't expect me to discuss this sort of high-falutin nonsense. I know when a thing 's wrong and I know when a thing 's right.

BILL. You 're uncommonly lucky, then.

MRS. WENHAM. However, I won't say anything more about it now. We 've got other things to think about at the moment. But really, Hugo, really I do think it 's disgraceful what you 've done.

HUGO (*shrugging his shoulders*). I 'm sorry.

MRS. WENHAM. As if that made any difference. The point is : what are we going to do now ? You, I, your father, every one ?

(MR. GRAY *enters while she is speaking.* MRS. WENHAM *sees him.*)

Perhaps you can help to answer that question, Mr. Gray. What are we going to do ? What *are* we going to do ?

MR. GRAY. Well, as a matter of fact, that was just what I was coming to ask of you, Mrs. Wenham. I 've just been having a talk with your husband, and he tells me that he means to write to the papers about what 's happened.

MRS. WENHAM. You mean, about their coming back ?

(MR. GRAY *nods.*)

But what on earth for ? Is he mad ?

MR. GRAY. That 's what I said, of course. But he declares it 's a matter of principle. He can't go on sponsoring the untruth that 's in the book. But, as I said to him : ' My dear Wenham,' I said . . .

BILL. Bow, wow, bow ! (*With perfect gravity of manner.*)

MR. GRAY. What 's that ?

BILL. ' My dear Wenham,' you said. And what then ? I haven't been so amused for weeks.

HUGO. Oh, for God's sake, Bill, be quiet.

BILL. Mayn't I even be amused ?

MR. GRAY. Well, as I was saying : ' My dear Wenham,' I said . . .

MRS. WENHAM. But we simply must prevent him from sending that letter. Listen, Hugo, you 've got to help us. You simply must.

HUGO. I 'll do what I can.

MRS. WENHAM. Oh, how stupid it all is. Too utterly stupid ! (*In an outburst of exasperation.*)

BILL. But that 's just the beauty of it. That 's . . .

HUGO. Come on, Bill. Let 's come and have breakfast. (*Laying his hand on* BILL'S *shoulder.*)

BILL. All right. I 'll come quietly.

(*As they approach the door into the hall* MR. WENHAM *enters.*)

MR. WENHAM. Ah, good morning, dear boy. Good morning, Mr. Hamblin.

HUGO. Morning, father.

MR. WENHAM. Where are you off to ?

HUGO. Going to have some breakfast.

MR. WENHAM. What, hasn't Mr. Hamblin had his breakfast yet ?

HUGO. No, we went for a turn in the garden first. Come on, Bill.

BILL. You see, I make such a hoggish mess now when I eat. So I prefer doing it when nobody 's there. I daresay the best thing would be if I had a little trough made for myself and ate off the floor. That would . . .

HUGO. Oh, come on, Bill. (*He leads him out.*)

MR. WENHAM (*advancing into the room and sitting down*). It really is too dreadful about that poor

young man. Blinded like that, by the stupidest
accident. And what makes it worse, he's so
terribly . . . so terribly resentful about it. So
bitter. That self-laceration . . . (*Passes his hand
over his forehead.*) Oh, dear . . .

MRS. WENHAM. Mr. Gray tells me, dear, that you
mean to write a letter to the papers about . . . well,
about all this.

MR. WENHAM. Yes, one was just coming to tell
you.

MRS. WENHAM. But is it necessary, John? Isn't
it . . . isn't it simply madness?

MR. GRAY. Madness. I entirely agree with Mrs.
Wenham.

MR. WENHAM. But don't you see, dear, one's in a
false position. One's countenancing an untruth.
It's a question of scientific good faith.

MRS. WENHAM. Oh, if it's only a question of
science . . .

MR. WENHAM. Besides, one's actually obtaining
money on false pretences. Every time somebody
buys a copy of the book, one's committing a
swindle. Can't you see? One *must* write that
letter.

MRS. WENHAM. But, John, have you thought of the
consequences?

MR. GRAY. Yes, the consequences, my dear Wenham.

MRS. WENHAM. They'll make a laughing-stock of
you, an absolute laughing-stock. John, I beg
you—please don't send that letter.

MR. WENHAM. But, dear, there's a principle at
stake.

MRS. WENHAM. They'll be so horrible and beastly
about it.

MR. WENHAM. Perhaps they will be.   But after all, if it's right . . .

MRS. WENHAM.   But it isn't right to go and destroy your whole life like this, deliberately.   It isn't right.   And destroy it for what ?   For nothing. For a lot of wretched ghosts.   Because even if they did exist, what difference would it make ?

MR. WENHAM.   But surely, my dear . . .

MRS. WENHAM (*cutting him short*).   Yes, what difference ?   Oh, I believe in the life to come and all that.   I 'm a good Christian.   I go to church every Sunday.   But I 've got my house to look after, and the children to think about, and you. I simply haven't got time for ghosts and séances and all the rest.   I simply don't want to be interfered with by them, if you see what I mean.

MR. GRAY.   How I agree with you, Mrs. Wenham ! Religion is a wonderful thing in its proper place. But it should never be allowed to invade the sanctities of private life.   Never.   That's *my* opinion.

MRS. WENHAM.   You 've got no right to destroy real things for the sake of what isn't real. You 've got no right to murder your happiness like this.

MR. WENHAM.   But, dear, it isn't a question of happiness now.   It 's a question of honesty and good faith.   After all, one can't think only of one's own feelings.

MRS. WENHAM.   I quite agree.   But what about other people's feelings, John ?   Think a little about my feelings, think a little of the children's feelings.

MR. GRAY.   Think a little of *my* feelings.

MRS. WENHAM.   Think of the boys at school, how

they 'll be teased and jeered at when your letter 's published. Why should *we* be made to suffer ?

MR. GRAY. Precisely.

MRS. WENHAM. It isn't only your own happiness that you 're murdering.

MR. WENHAM (*gets up and walks restlessly about the room*). Do you think it will be as bad as all that ?

MRS. WENHAM. I 'm sure it will.

MR. GRAY. Worse even, I should say.

MR. WENHAM (*sitting down again, after a silence*). Still one *must* do what 's right. Oh, if only one hadn't had the idea of publishing that book ! But Capes seemed so perfectly all right. One could have sworn . . . Oh, God ! I don't know, I don't know . . .

MRS. WENHAM (*insinuatingly*). Suppose you just quietly withdrew the book, John. Wouldn't that be enough ?

MR. WENHAM. What difference would that make ?

MRS. WENHAM. I should have thought it would make a great deal of difference. If people couldn't buy the book any more . . .

MR. WENHAM. But the lie would have been published just the same, and I shouldn't have contradicted it. It 's a question of telling the truth.

MR. GRAY. Quite, quite. But not rashly, never rashly, my dear Wenham. Writing a letter to the papers—that 's simply foolhardiness.

MRS. WENHAM. Mr. Gray 's quite right, dear.

MR. GRAY. One should never do anything without carefully thinking it over first.

MR. WENHAM. Not even tell the truth ?

MR. GRAY. Oh, the truth before everything, of course. *Magna est veritas*, as we used to say. But there are good ways and bad ways of telling it, there are auspicious moments and inauspicious moments. I think you'll agree with me, Mrs. Wenham?

MRS. WENHAM. Entirely.

MR. GRAY. And above all, anything like rashness, anything like precipitation must be avoided. It's like having a puncture when you're driving a car. If you're going at sixty miles an hour and your tyre bursts, it's dangerous, it's extremely dangerous. But a small hole, a gradual leak, that's quite harmless. It seems to me that that's what we ought to aim at in this case—just a very gradual leaking out of the truth. Because if it all came out at once, with a bang—well, really, I don't know what would happen. The book's selling with such a momentum, the publicity's at full throttle—everything's fairly whizzing along. And then, pop! You go and explode the truth on us. Why, there'd be the most hideous smash-up. Terrible! Of course, I'm not thinking about myself—though naturally it doesn't do any publisher much good to be openly made a fool of. I'm thinking of you. (*He pats* MR. WENHAM *on the shoulder.*)

MR. WENHAM (*shrinking deeper into his chair*). Most kind, I'm sure, but——

MR. GRAY. Yes, my dear Wenham, I'm thinking of you. *Your* reputation, *your* happiness, *your* position in the world, *your* . . .

> (*He breaks off at the sight of* HUBERT CAPES, *who has entered from the hall and is standing hesitating on the threshold. In a portentous tone.*)

Good morning, Mr. Capes.

HUBERT (*nervously*). Oh . . . Good morning. I

was just looking for Mr. Wenham. Good morning, Mr. Wenham. But it doesn't matter. I'll
wait till later on, when you're alone. (*He makes
as if to retire.*)

MR. GRAY. Wait a minute, please, Mr. Capes. I'd
like a word with you. We'd all like a word with
you, I think.

> (MRS. WENHAM *shrugs her shoulders and,
> turning away, leans against the mantelpiece.
> Huddled in his chair* MR. WENHAM *says
> nothing.*)

MR. GRAY (*bullyingly*). In fact we'd like several
words.

HUBERT (*very nervously*). Well, I'm sure I shall be
delighted.

MR. GRAY. I'm sure you *won't* be delighted. I certainly don't *want* you to be delighted. Because,
young man, I consider you a low, dirty swindler.

HUBERT. No, really. I . . . I . . . Mr. Wenham, I
beg you . . .

MR. WENHAM. After all, Gray, we don't know, we
can't judge . . .

MR. GRAY. Leave this to me, Wenham. (*Turning
back to* HUBERT, *thoroughly enjoying his righteous
indignation.*) I repeat, sir, a low, dirty swindler.
And I will add, a heartless cheat.

HUBERT (*plaintively indignant*). But . . . but this
is dreadful. And if you knew how ill I felt. That
shock I had last night . . . It's monstrous.

MR. GRAY. Monstrous. I quite agree. Exploiting
the grief of a bereaved father, playing on the most
sacred feelings for your own base and venial—I
mean venal—purposes. Absolutely monstrous.

HUBERT. But it's not true, Mr. Gray. I never did
that. I swear.

MR. GRAY.   That 's it, swear away.   Add perjury to cheating.

HUBERT.   But it wasn't cheating.   I never did anything that wasn't absolutely straight.   Did I, Mr. Wenham ?

MR. WENHAM.   Well, certainly one never . . . one never detected anything wrong.

MR. GRAY.   Quite so.   He was a very clever cheat. That 's all *that* proves.

HUBERT.   But on my word of honour, Mr. Gray . . .

MR. GRAY (*laughing*).   On your word of honour ! That 's good, that 's very good.   Did you hear that, Mrs. Wenham ?   On his word of honour.

HUBERT.   But it 's true.   Oh, Mrs. Wenham, do believe me.

MRS. WENHAM (*shrugging her shoulders without turning round*).   What does it matter if I believe you or not ?   It won't make any difference to what 's happened . . . to what 's going to happen.

HUBERT.   Yes, what *is* going to happen ?   What will people say about me if this gets known ?

MR. GRAY.   They 'll say exactly what I 've said, young man.   That you 're an impudent and heartless swindler.   Do you realise what you 've let the unfortunate Mr. Wenham in for ?   Do you realise ?

HUBERT.   It was a mistake, I swear.   I simply can't think how it happened.   The messages were so clear and definite . . . weren't they, Mr. Wenham ?

MR. GRAY.   Oh, stop that stupid canting !   Clear and definite, indeed !   Clear and definite swindling.   The man ought to be horse-whipped, don't you agree, Mrs. Wenham ?   Soundly horse-whipped and then kicked out of the house.   Do you hear what I say, sir ?   (*He advances menacingly towards* HUBERT, *who cowers away in abject terror.*)

HUBERT. No. Don't. Please. I'm so ill.

MR. WENHAM (*who has risen, speaking at the same time as* HUBERT). No, Gray, no.

(*While this has been going on,* HUGO *has entered and has advanced unnoticed into the room. He is already quite close to the shrinking* HUBERT *when he makes his presence known.*)

HUGO. But what on earth is happening here?

(HUBERT *turns round with a start, sees* HUGO *standing over him and immediately bolts behind the table.*)

HUBERT. No, no, please. Oh, it isn't fair. If you knew how bad my heart was. Really, I swear.

HUGO (*looking round in astonishment*). But has every one gone mad, or what?

HUBERT (*reassured, emerging from behind the table*). Goodness! I thought . . . my nerves are in such an awful state . . .

HUGO. Did you imagine I was going to set on you?

HUBERT. No, no. It was just my nerves. I'm sorry I was so foolish. Let's talk about something else.

HUGO. But I'm afraid I must talk about this. Because if you imagined I was going to attack you, you must also imagine that I have some reason for attacking you.

MR. GRAY. It's his guilty conscience, Mr. Wenham. That's the reason. The man's a common swindler.

HUGO. But I don't agree with you, Mr. Gray. I don't believe for a moment that there's been any fraud.

HUBERT. There, you see !

MR. GRAY. No fraud ? (*Spoken simultaneously with* HUBERT'S *words*.) But come, my dear sir, come. You're alive, aren't you ? You're not a departed spirit ?

HUGO. But that's only a detail.

MR. GRAY. Rather an important detail, I should have thought.

HUGO. Only from my point of view, not from Mr. Capes's.

MR. GRAY. But the fellow professed to be bringing messages from you in the next world.

HUGO. Well, it was just a little mistake, that's all. He was bringing them from me in this world. Do remember that spiritualism's only a theory for interpreting certain facts. There are other theories that fit the facts just as well—better, even. What's important is the facts.

MR. GRAY. You mean the concertina and all that sort of thing ?

HUGO. Yes ; and clairvoyance and telepathy and so on—those are the facts. If you like to say that they have something to do with dead people, you may. But it's purely a matter of taste. You can have all the facts and no belief in ghosts. Mediums who work for non-spiritualists never dream of having anything to do with ghosts. Whereas those who work for spiritualists—like you, father —well, naturally, they tend to find ghosts everywhere—swarms of them. It's only natural.

MR. WENHAM. Then you think that our young friend here . . .

HUGO. . . . is perfectly genuine. Only a bit mistaken in his interpretations. I hope you'll excuse my talking about you like this, Mr. Capes.

HUBERT. But of course. I'm so grateful for your support. I couldn't bear my honour being questioned. It's never happened before.

HUGO. Well, there's no reason why it should happen again if you stick to facts and avoid theories. You see, Mr. Gray, he's what's called a psychic subject—a man with certain special gifts. However, as he's always worked for spiritualists, he tends to attribute everything he does to ghosts. I mean, if a bell rings at a distance it's Napoleon or Joan of Arc. Or suppose the concertina plays something out of *Figaro*—then it's my ghost playing, because I happened to like the tune. But it isn't my ghost. It's Mr. Capes himself.

MR. GRAY. There, didn't I say so?

HUGO. Not the ordinary, waking Mr. Capes. Mr. Capes's unconscious mind influenced by my mind and using some sort of ectoplasm stuff to play the concertina with.

MR. GRAY. That's a bit far-fetched, isn't it?

HUGO. But you can take photographs of it, you know. Streams of ectoplasm guttering out of the medium's ears, or nose, or mouth. Great oozing tentacles of it, like the arms of an octopus. It makes the ghosts quite superfluous and unnecessary.

HUBERT. I can't quite agree with you there, of course. The spirits make use of the ectoplasm. (*Embarrassed*) At least they do in most cases. Don't they, Mr. Wenham?

MR. WENHAM. Well, one thought they did. One imagined . . . but I don't know now, I don't know. (*Despairingly*.)

MR. GRAY. Then you really think there was no fraud in any of those messages?

P

HUGO. No fraud; only a misinterpretation. You
see, father, you'd all got it so firmly into your
heads that I was dead. Anything Mr. Capes
extracted out of my mind by long-distance thought-
reading you immediately put down as a communication from my departed spirit.

MR. GRAY. But do you think he really did get
things out of your mind?

HUGO. Think? I know he did. I spent most of
last night reading your book, father. It made me
feel quite uncomfortable sometimes, as though I'd
been living all this time with somebody's eye at
the keyhole.

HUBERT. I'm most awfully sorry.

HUGO. It seemed so extraordinary that you should
know so much about me, father—you of all people
—forgive me for that.

MR. WENHAM. Yes, I of all people.

HUGO. You know, it's an extraordinarily good
book. (*Looking at his father while he speaks.*)

MR. GRAY (*with an air of proprietorship*). I'm glad
you think so, Mr. Wenham.

HUGO. I'd no idea you could write so well, father.
I really congratulate you.

  (MR. WENHAM *shakes his head and makes a
  gesture of negation.*)

MR. GRAY. You knew, of course, that it's been one
of the great successes of the publishing season?

HUGO. No.

MR. GRAY. Sixteen thousand copies already sold.

HUGO (*whistles*). Whew!

MR. GRAY. At a guinea each, mark you.

HUGO. Well, there's an idea for a career. Why not
take up spiritualism? I'd been wondering what
I should do now.

MRS. WENHAM (*turning round sharply*). Listen, Hugo, it's time to speak seriously. All this talk about ghosts and ectoplasm and scientific theories may be very interesting. But it's out of place, it's beside the point. Your father is proposing to write to the papers to say that you've come back, that the book was all a mistake. . . .

HUBERT (*horrified*). You are not, Mr. Wenham! But it would be the ruin of me. It's too terrible, it's . . .

MRS. WENHAM (*coldly*). Perhaps you'll allow me to finish what I was saying, Mr. Capes. What we want to know now, Hugo, is not whether there are such things as ghosts, but whether your father still means to send that letter.

HUGO. Do you, father?

MR. WENHAM (*after a long pause, miserably*). One can't countenance an untruth, can one?

HUGO. But, after all, it isn't an untruth . . . not really. All the phenomena were perfectly genuine.

HUBERT. Absolutely, I swear it.

MR. WENHAM. But the interpretation—that was wrong. The world of light . . .

HUGO. Oh, I wouldn't bother about the world of light.

MR. WENHAM. I made statements which weren't true. One must do what's right.

MR. GRAY. But think of the consequences, my dear Wenham.

MRS. WENHAM. For all of us. Think of the children at school.

HUBERT. Think of me.

MRS. WENHAM. You know how malicious little boys are, how they'd jeer.

HUGO.   And then think of poor Bill.   It'll be so bad for him if you mix him up in a lot of excitement and publicity.

HUBERT.   And it would be absolute ruin for me.

HUGO.   Bill's nerves are in such a state.

MR. GRAY.   And you know, we can easily withdraw the book.   Just make it quietly disappear from the bookshops.

MRS. WENHAM.   And then when the publicity has died down . . .

HUGO.   You could write a second book, more cautious, so as to prepare the way.

MRS. WENHAM.   And then . . .

MR. GRAY.   Very, very gradually let the truth leak out.

HUBERT.   Or not leak at all.   Perhaps that would really be better.

MR. WENHAM (*getting up distracted*).   I'm sorry, one can't stay.   One's got to be alone.   (*He moves towards the door.*)

MRS. WENHAM.   But John, what about that letter?

MR. WENHAM.   Oh, I don't know, one can't decide. One must think it over.

MR. GRAY.   If you'll take my advice, Wenham . . .

MR. WENHAM.   No, don't give it me now, Gray. Please don't.   I don't think I could stand it.   (*He hurries out through the door into the hall.*)

MR. GRAY.   Do you think it would be a good thing if I followed him and—you know—rubbed in my arguments a little?

HUGO.   No.   No.   Leave the poor man in peace for a moment.

MRS. WENHAM.   But perhaps later on, if the matter's still undecided . . .

MR. GRAY.   Yes, I'll rub it in.

MRS. WENHAM. Well, meanwhile one can only wait and hope. You 'll withdraw the book anyhow, won't you, Mr. Gray ?

MR. GRAY. It 's the first thing I 'll attend to when I get back to London. Which reminds me (*looking at his watch*)—nearly eleven. Perhaps I ought to go and pack my bag if I 'm going to catch that five to twelve train.

MRS. WENHAM. And I must go and talk to the cook. Heaven and earth may pass away, but dinner 's got to be ordered.

(MRS. WENHAM *goes out, followed by* MR. GRAY. *There is a silence.*)

HUGO (*shaking his head*). Well. It 's a bad business, a thoroughly bad business.

HUBERT. It would have been still worse, so far as I 'm concerned, if you hadn't come and taken my part. That was very kind of you, Hugo—I mean Mr. Wenham. I beg your pardon. I 've been so used to calling you Hugo all this time. One 's on more affectionate terms with the spirits, somehow. There 's not so much etiquette on the other side.

HUGO. Well, I 'm not a stickler for it even on this side.

HUBERT. Oh, dear, if only your father hadn't written that book ! It 's really terrible to think that a single mistake can ruin one's whole career. (*More clerically*) Besides, there 's the Cause to think of. It would be awful if one had done anything, even accidentally, to injure the Cause.

HUGO. Oh, the Cause 'll be all right. Don't you bother about the Cause, Mr. Capes. It 's as safe as the Bank of England. Safer really, when you come to think of it. Another war might easily bust the Bank ; but it could do nothing but good to spiritualism.

HUBERT (*unctuously*).   At the great crises of history the great human truths have always come into their own.

HUGO.   Quite, quite.   (*After a little pause*) Tell me, as a matter of curiosity—was it genuine *every* time ?

HUBERT (*indignantly*).   Genuine ?   How can you ask such a question ?

HUGO.   Come now, don't take it badly.   I know it was genuine most of the time.   But weren't there occasions when . . . well, when the phenomena had to be helped out a little ?

HUBERT.   Certainly not.

HUGO.   Strictly between ourselves, you know.

HUBERT.   I 'm ready to swear.

HUGO.   No, please don't do that.

HUBERT.   Every time—it was genuine every time. Even those messages for Enid.

HUGO.   Which messages for Enid ?

HUBERT (*embarrassed*).   Well . . . it 's rather difficult to explain.

HUGO (*looking at his watch*).   Yes, quite.   I really ought to go and see how poor old Bill 's getting on.

HUBERT (*laying a hand on* HUGO'S *arm, as the latter moves towards the library door*).   Just a minute, Mr. Wenham, I 'd like to talk to you for a moment. About those messages—about Enid.

HUGO.   Fire away, then.

HUBERT.   Well . . . (*He coughs nervously.*)   It 's like this.   You were engaged to Enid.   You don't mind my being personal, I hope ?

HUGO.   Not *very* much.

HUBERT.   You see, I know so many things about you.   As though you were a historical character, if you see what I mean.   It's strange, isn't it?

(HUGO *nods, making a wry face.*)

Well, as I say, you were engaged to Enid.   Poor girl!   The news of your death—I mean, what we thought was your death—naturally, it was a terrible shock to her.   Terrible.   (*Clerically*) It would have made your heart bleed to see her at that time.

HUGO.   I'm glad I didn't.   (*He gets up and takes one or two turns up and down the room.*)   Was she really upset?

HUBERT.   I was afraid she might do something desperate.

HUGO.   What do you mean?

HUBERT.   Kill herself, even.   She confessed to me afterwards that she'd actually made up her mind. And she'd have done it, I believe, if it hadn't been for the new faith and hope that came to her with the séances.   (*Embarrassed*) Well, in the circumstances it did look as though . . . I mean, they did seem to justify faith and hope . . .

HUGO.   Quite, quite.

HUBERT.   You understand?

(HUGO *nods.*)

And then I did my best, of course, to help her. (*Unctuously*) It was my duty; it's what I'm called and appointed to do—to help people in cases like this.   Besides, my heart bled for her.

(*Unseen by* HUBERT, HUGO *makes a grimace.*)

HUBERT.   I talked to her, I tried to console her. And then . . . it's difficult to describe exactly how it came about . . . but gradually, little by little, well, our feelings began to change . . .

without our being aware at first.   You know how it happens.

HUGO (*looking greatly relieved*).   Yes, I know how it happens.   You fell in love with her, in fact.   And she fell in love with you, I take it.   Well, why not ?

HUBERT (*taken aback*).   Why not ?   But, after all, you were engaged.

HUGO.   But only in a previous existence.

HUBERT.   I . . . I thought you 'd have minded. I mean, neither of us would have dreamt of . . . caring for one another, if it hadn't been for certain . . . certain . . . well, we thought they were messages from your spirit.   Messages that encouraged us to . . . to . . . you see what I mean ?

HUGO.   Oh, perfectly.

HUBERT.   Such definite messages.

HUGO.   I 'm sure they were.

HUBERT.   And as it was really a question of saving her life . . .

HUGO.   But why apologise like this ?   I can only wish you happiness.

HUBERT.   But I wouldn't dream of standing in your way now.

HUGO.   You 're not standing in my way.

HUBERT (*growing almost desperate*).   I mean, you have certain rights, certain prior claims.

HUGO.   But what a way to speak of it, man !   As though we were discussing house property !

HUBERT.   What I meant to say was that I feel it as a duty.   I 'm ready to renounce . . .

HUGO.   But, damn it, I don't ask you to renounce.

HUBERT.   But I couldn't accept such sacrifices.   I simply couldn't . . .

(*The door opens and* ENID *enters.* HUBERT *sees her at once.*)

Oh !

HUGO (*who has his back to the door, turns round*).
Ah ! here 's Enid. (*His tone and expression are
positively jolly. He has been steadily brightening
throughout the previous conversation.*) Ought I
to start congratulating . . . (*He is advancing
towards her, but checks his movement; his words
are abruptly frozen on his lips by the expression of
stony misery on* ENID'S *face. She is dressed in
black.*) I'm sorry, Enid.

ENID (*walks slowly into the middle of the room and
sits down before answering*). Sorry, Hugo ?
What for ?

HUGO. Well, I don't know. *You 'll* have to tell me
that. Sorry for being here, I suppose. For not
being dead.

ENID. Oh, if only *I* were dead.

HUBERT. But you ought to be feeling thankful,
Enid. It 's really a miracle.

ENID (*with sudden anger*). Oh, be quiet, Hubert !
Bleating away like a beastly little clergyman—it 's
disgusting ! And the hypocrisy of it ! Talking
about thankfulness and miracles so as to avoid
telling the real truth. Anything to avoid the
truth. (*She checks herself.*) I 'm sorry. But
you did drive me to it. Thankfulness indeed !
(*She laughs hysterically.*) That was really too
much. (*She pulls herself together once more.*)
Listen, Hugo, the truth 's got to be told. I know
Hubert won't tell it. And I rather doubt if you 'll
tell it. Besides, you don't know it all—only your
part of it. I 'm the only one who knows the whole
of it. And I 'm the only one who 's got the courage to tell it. You 're cowards, you know, both
of you. Perhaps all men are a bit cowardly when

it comes to facing the truth about feelings. And perhaps it's also because neither of you has suffered. You've only inflicted suffering. I'm the one it's been inflicted on. That's why I can tell the truth and you can't. Because I'm not ashamed. One isn't ashamed of suffering pain. One's only ashamed of inflicting it. You inflicted it. So you're ashamed, and it's that which prevents you from telling the truth. You're cowards through shame. Isn't that it?

HUGO. Yes, perhaps there's something in that.

HUBERT. Well, personally, I don't know of anything I've done that I need be ashamed of.

ENID (*with bitter irony*). No, of course you don't. Tell me, Hugo, don't you think I'm right? Isn't one always ashamed of inflicting pain, even when it isn't one's fault and one really can't help it? I mean, it wasn't your fault that you couldn't bear me. It wasn't your fault that you had that kind of instinctive physical horror of me. (*Her voice trembles.*)

HUGO (*greatly distressed*). Enid, don't! It's horrible. You're lacerating yourself.

ENID (*with a kind of laugh*). There! You see? You're shirking it again. You're ashamed of having hurt me, and therefore you haven't got the courage to tell the truth, or even to hear the truth. Because it *is* the truth, isn't it? Admit it. It *is* the truth.

HUGO (*after a pause*). Well, it's nearly the truth, I suppose.

ENID (*smiling sadly*). ' Nearly the truth.' You're getting braver, Hugo. Nearly the truth. And yet you liked me, in spite of everything. We were friends, weren't we? Even though I did bully you.   Do you remember, you once said I ought to wear a stiff collar and cuffs like a nurse ?   Because I treated you as though you were a typhoid patient. Poor Hugo !   I 'm sorry.   But you liked me all the same.   Perhaps just because of the cuffs and collar.   Secretly you rather enjoyed being bullied, didn't you ?

HUGO.   Did I ?

ENID.   Yes.   But you hated it at the same time. And the hatred was made worse because of that kind of horror, that physical horror.   Oh, I knew it all, I understood it all.   And yet I 'd forgotten, or rather I 'd invented another past for myself, because I didn't like the real past.   I 'm a coward too, you see.   Yes, a coward and a liar.   Why are we all such cowards and liars, Hugo ?   I believe there 's a cowardly lie at the bottom of every soul. Perhaps there 's got to be.   Perhaps it 's the only condition on which we can ever be happy.   Do you know, I 've been lying to myself about you ever since you went away—or at least ever since we thought you were dead.   Making a myth about you and our relations with each other. And I 'd done it so successfully that last night, just before I went to sleep, I decided to come to you in the morning and suggest—can you guess what ?

(HUGO *shakes his head.*)

That we should go away together and start a new life—like people in the movies !   (*Laughs.*) Luckily I saw through the lie when I woke up this morning.   Seven o'clock is a very truthful hour. What would you have done if I hadn't seen through it.   I mean, supposing I 'd come and asked you to take me—what *would* you have done?

(*She leans forward with an ironical smile and yet desperately hopeful.*)

HUGO. Well . . . (*He hesitates.*) I really don't know. I mean . . .

ENID (*throwing herself back with a laugh that is the more mocking for covering a real disappointment*). You mean that you really know quite well, but don't want to hurt my feelings. Thank you for being a coward and liar again. It 's well meant, I know. But all the same, if it had come to the point, you 'd have told me to go to hell, wouldn't you ?

HUGO. Come now, really !

ENID. Well, at any rate, you 'd have run away again and left me here in hell, just as you did last time. Wouldn't you ?

(*There is a pause.* HUGO *nods, slowly.*)
Yes, of course you would. Why should you want to stay in hell ?

HUGO. But is it hell, Enid ? I thought you . . . you . . . well, that you 'd been happy. I mean, Capes was saying something to me just now . . .

ENID (*in a deliberately hard, flippant tone*). Oh, was he ? What was he saying ? That we 'd slept together ?

HUBERT (*genuinely shocked, as well as embarrassed*). Enid, how can you !

ENID (*mocking*). Yes, how *can* I ? Isn't it shocking, to talk about the things we all do—isn't it disgustingly immoral ?

HUBERT (*who has had time to adjust his face and manner*). It was the desecration I minded, the making light of something sacred.

ENID (*springing to her feet*). Something sacred ? Oh, you 're horrible, you 're disgusting ! Go away, you beast! (*She strikes him in the face.*)

    (HUBERT *shrinks away, astonished, terrified, abject.*)

Go away! Get out of my sight. (*She makes as if to strike him again.* HUGO *lays a hand on her arm.*)

HUBERT. No, Enid, no.

ENID (*turning away from* HUBERT, *and walking back to her seat*). All right. But tell him to go away. I can't bear to see him.

HUGO. You 'd better go, Capes.

HUBERT (*who has recovered from his first shock of terror and has become plaintively the sick man, brutally outraged. He keeps his hand pressed to his side.*) It 's my heart. You know, I nearly died. That shock . . . Mediums have been known to pass over when they 're woken up like that. I think I 'll go and lie down. (*He totters out.*)

HUGO (*comes back from shutting the door after showing* HUBERT *out, and sits down beside* ENID. *Silence. He lays his hand on* ENID'S *arm*). I 'm sorry, Enid, I wish I could do something.

ENID. There isn't anything you can do. Nobody can do anything. I wish I were dead. What 's the point of this stupid body going on when everything else is finished?

HUGO. But everything isn't finished, Enid.

ENID. Yes, it is, and if I had the courage, I 'd finish myself too. But I haven't got the courage.

    (*Enter from the library* MR. WENHAM *leading* BILL.)

MR. WENHAM. Here 's Mr. Hamblin, Hugo. He was wondering what had become of you.

BILL. Wondering ? I was damning your eyes.
You really are disgusting, Hugo. Marooning me
there alone in the library, not knowing how to get
out, not knowing where the bell was.

HUGO. But you said you wanted to rest, Bill.

BILL. Yes, but I didn't say I wanted to be dumped
like a bit of luggage and forgotten about. You
really might think of me sometimes.

HUGO. But damn it all, Bill, I do think of
you.

BILL. Every now and then, when it suits your con-
venience.

HUGO. But you know you don't like me to be hanging round you too attentively.

BILL. I don't like your beastly patronising bedside
manner, that's all. All that sort of ' How 's-the-
little-patient ' business and ' We 'll be up and
about again next week.' It 's intolerable ; I don't
want to have any of your damned encouragement.
It 's an impertinence, it 's an insult.

MR. WENHAM. But you can't expect Hugo to talk
discouragingly.

BILL. No, all I ask him to do is to talk naturally—
as he used to talk before this happened. (*He
touches his spectacles.*) Like one normal human
being to another. But then I 'm not a normal
human being now. I 'm maimed. I 'm a monster.
So I suppose I can't expect people to talk naturally to me. Just because I happened to have
fallen face first into a cactus-bush, am I to be
patronised and insulted for the rest of my life ?
Well, I suppose I shall get used to it in time. But
I must say, at present I find it pretty difficult to
swallow. And then to be left like an old Glad-
stone bag in a corner of the room. And to be

helpless, helpless, utterly helpless ... (*He clenches his fists, his voice trembles.*)

HUGO.   But, after all, Bill, you 'll soon learn to be independent.

BILL.   Oh, be quiet, Hugo! Be quiet! I will not be triumphed over and insulted. All this loathsome bedside encouragement—it 's just people triumphing over the helpless. No healthy man can see a sick man without wanting to triumph over him. It may be disguised as Christian kindness. But it 's always triumph underneath. (*Putting his hand to his collar.*) It 's hot in here, it 's stifling. I think it 's partly the effect of being in the dark. As though one were inside an oven. Horrible. Will you take me out into the garden for a bit, Hugo?

HUGO.   Well, if you 'd like me to, if you don't think I shall just get on your nerves again.

ENID.   Would you care to come with me, Mr. Hamblin? I was going out in any case.

BILL.   Well, that 's kind of you. You 're sure it 's not too much of a bore.

ENID.   The pinks are all out, you know. (*She takes his arm.*) The scent of them is simply too delicious——

BILL.   Well, at any rate I can still enjoy that.

ENID.   And then, how lovely flowers feel! Pinks are feathery; so are cornflowers. The roses are like a very smooth, cool skin. And pansies are satiny —which is rather surprising, I always think, because pansies *look* like velvet.

BILL.   Yes, that 's true.

ENID (*opening the door*). A little step. That 's it.

BILL (*turning back on the threshold*). Hugo?

HUGO.   Yes, Bill?

BILL. I 'm sorry I was so awful just now.

HUGO. Oh, that didn't matter, Bill.

(BILL *and* ENID *go out.*)

MR. WENHAM (*after a pause*). To see and yet be utterly in the dark, groping. In a certain sense, I wish . . . I almost wish I were physically blind, like poor young Hamblin. If one could suffer physically— perhaps it would be a kind of relief. At least it would be something definite to resist and be resigned to. It would be something one could be— well, it sounds a big word . . . one could be heroic about. Oedipus put out his own eyes. I can understand that. He wanted to match his spiritual blindness and perplexity with blindness in the flesh. Yes, I can understand that, now.

HUGO. But come, father, you 're taking everything much too tragically.

MR. WENHAM. No, that 's the trouble—I can't take it tragically enough. If only one *were* Oedipus ! But one isn't. One 's just—just an elderly manufacturer of office equipment wondering whether he 'll have the courage to do what he ought to do.

HUGO. You mean, about that letter to the press ?

MR. WENHAM (*nodding*). Yes.

HUGO. But honestly, father, I don't think you ought to send it, for Alice's sake to start with.

MR. WENHAM. Yes, I know. If it were physical pain, one could bear it alone. It would be entirely one's own private affair. But this . . . this can't be kept exclusively to oneself. And yet one *ought* to write that letter, one *ought* to publish the truth.

HUGO. Be careful, father. You 're looking for excuses to suffer, you 're trying to find justifications. Are any of those excuses and justifications

good enough to allow you to make other people
suffer ?

MR. WENHAM.   Were your excuses and justifications
good enough, Hugo ?

HUGO.   Perhaps they weren't—though I feel that it
would have been the sin against the Holy Ghost
if I hadn't done the cruel thing I did.

MR. WENHAM.   But perhaps it would be the sin
against the Holy Ghost in this case too.   Because
I feel I *ought* to suffer.   It's a question of—how
shall I put it ?—a question of concentrating a kind
of—a kind of diffused misery and perplexity in a
single focus—killing one kind of pain with
another sharper pain.   One could bear the pain ;
but the diffused misery—that's unbearable.   Unbearable.   It's as though . . . as though all
one's light had gone suddenly dark.   They are
all gone into the world of light, and I alone sit
lingering here.   But perhaps they haven't gone
into the world of light.   Perhaps there isn't a
world of light for them to go into ?   Do you
remember those other verses later on in the poem ?

> He that hath found some fledged bird's nest may
>   know
>   At first sight if the bird be flown ;
> But what fair well or grove he sings in now,
>   That is to him unknown.

But if there isn't a well or a grove or a bird to sing?
It's like a sudden darkness, it's like being blind
. . . blind in a desert.   It isn't pain.   It's just
emptiness and dryness and darkness.   Just blindness in a desert.

HUGO (*deliberately brutal*).   In a word, I spoilt your
theory, and you'd rather have your theory than me.

Q

MR. WENHAM. But that's not true, that's a cruel thing to say.

HUGO. But after all, it's natural enough. In a sense, the theory was always much more real than I was. So far as you're concerned, father, I've never really been there at all. I was a kind of ghost while I was alive . . . more of a ghost really than when I was dead. There was always a gulf fixed between us.

MR. WENHAM. Yes, there was always a gulf. (*Slowly, nodding his head.*)

HUGO. I suppose there's a gulf between most fathers and their sons.

MR. WENHAM. And yet, God knows, it wasn't from any lack of interest or . . . or affection on one's own part. Somehow, you know, it was easier when you were away, when we thought you were —well, that you had passed over. One seemed to be so much more intimate with you, dear boy.

HUGO. Thanks to young Capes. His messages made the ghost more real than the live man.

MR. WENHAM. But now the ghost has been made real, couldn't the live man be made real too ? I mean, this new intimacy—why shouldn't it go on ? One has never been much good at . . . well, at expressing one's feelings ; but that didn't prevent them from existing. They were always there, they are still there. All one's pride in you, dear boy, all one's . . . one's anxious solicitude, all one's . . . (*He hesitates for a long time—embarrassed*) one's love. (*He lays his hand for a moment, shyly, on* HUGO'S *knee. Awkwardly,* HUGO *touches his father's hand, then withdraws his own.*) And then I believe you really . . . well, you really care underneath, don't you ?

(HUGO *nods.*)

So why shouldn't we go on from where we were when you were away ? If I could feel that this thing had bridged the gulf I wouldn't mind anything else. If it had really given me back a son, I wouldn't care what it had taken away. Even if it had taken away the world of light. I shouldn't mind. I should even be glad. Don't you think we could go on, Hugo ? Don't you think it would be possible ?

HUGO. The gulf 's still there, father.

MR. WENHAM. But that bridge one threw across ?

HUGO. It only existed when I wasn't there, when you had Capes to build it.

MR. WENHAM. That intimacy ?

HUGO. It was only an intimacy in absence. Now that we 're together, can't you feel it ? There 's no contact any more, no flow between us.

MR. WENHAM. But perhaps that will pass, in time.

HUGO. No, it won't. It 'll never pass.

MR. WENHAM. One doesn't like to say ' Never.'

HUGO. But one 's got to say it, when it happens to be true.

MR. WENHAM. And you really think it 's true ?

HUGO. I know it 's true. And so do you, father, when you 're honest with yourself. (*Pause.*)

MR. WENHAM. Yes, I suppose that really I do know it 's true. Even last night one really knew. And this morning—yes, one was certain, one was really certain. Certain of the darkness, certain of being blind, blind in a desert. ' Dear beauteous death ' —do you remember that line in Vaughan's poem, ' Dear beauteous death, the jewel of the just ' ?

That's how I feel about it now. 'Dear beauteous death'! But meanwhile . . . meanwhile . . .

(*Enter* MR. GRAY, *loudly*. MR. WENHAM *looks round*.)

Oh God! (*An expression of distress passes over his face*.)

MR. GRAY. Ah, here you are, my dear Wenham. I was coming to say good-bye. It's been a most delightful visit. Most eventful too. What with all these resurrections and returns of prodigal sons —eh, Mr. Wenham. (*This is spoken jocularly to* HUGO, *who does not answer*.)

MR. WENHAM. Well, one hopes you'll come again in less . . . less exceptional circumstances.

MR. GRAY. That's most kind of you, I'm sure. And if I may be permitted to give you a word of good advice about that letter to the press . . .

MR. WENHAM (*hastily*). Do you know, I really think you ought to be going. I'll go and see if I can find Alice to come and say good-bye to you. (*He goes out through the door into the hall*.)

MR. GRAY (*turning eagerly to* HUGO *the moment the door is closed*). I hope you persuaded him to delay the publication of that wretched statement. What does he mean to do?

HUGO (*shrugging his shoulders*). I don't know. I don't think he knows himself.

MR. GRAY. It would be madness if he did send it —criminal madness. What I always say is, let sleeping dogs lie.

HUGO (*averting his face with an expression of contemptuous dislike*). Yes, and let lying dogs sleep.

MR. GRAY. I beg your pardon?

HUGO. Oh, nothing.

(*A silence.* HUGO *stands meditatively frowning.* MR. GRAY *looks at his watch.*)

MR. GRAY. It's getting rather late. I wonder if your stepmother . . .

HUGO (*with sudden decision*). Listen, the tree shall be known by its fruits—isn't that it?

MR. GRAY (*surprised*). I believe that's correct.

HUGO. Well, if so, then no fruits, no tree. Isn't that obvious? If I weren't here . . . tell me, is the car at the door?

MR. GRAY. I saw them putting my luggage into it.

HUGO. Good! Then let's make a bolt for it.

MR. GRAY. What do you mean?

HUGO. I'm off again.

MR. GRAY (*his face brightening*). You mean to say . . .?

HUGO. I'm better where I was—better anywhere rather than here. No fruits, no tree. And my God, what a tree it is!

MR. GRAY. But that's wonderful, my dear fellow! I mean we shall all be grieved to see you go. Terribly grieved. But still—well, it really is the best solution. I never ventured to suggest it; but of course I always thought . . .

HUGO (*laying a hand on his sleeve, cuts him short*). Listen. I shall need £500. Can you lend me that, Mr. Gray?

MR. GRAY (*alarmed*). Five hundred! That's a very big sum of money. (*His face brightening again*) But of course I could deduct it from your father's royalties on the book. (*Lavishly*) You shall have the money at once. More if you like. My dear chap, I'll make it a thousand.

HUGO. A thousand, then. I'm delighted. When can you let me have it?

MR. GRAY. This morning. We'll drive straight to the bank.

HUGO. Then come on. Quickly. Before my father comes back. (*He opens the hall door and puts his head out, listening.*) All clear. Sh-sh! Don't make a noise in the hall. (*They tiptoe out of the room. MR. WENHAM re-enters from the library. He glances in astonishment round the empty room.*)

MR. WENHAM. Hugo? Hugo?

(*The car is heard off. He crosses to the window and looks out. The car hoots.*)

Curtain

Printed in Great Britain by T. and A. CONSTABLE LTD.
at the University Press, Edinburgh